GLOBAL PERSPECTIVES ON SOCIAL ISSUES

GLOBAL PERSPECTIVES ON SOCIAL ISSUES
Education

by Rita J. Simon and Lisa Banks
with the assistance of Delene Bromirski

LEXINGTON BOOKS
Lanham · Boulder · New York · Oxford

ROWMAN & LITTLEFIELD PUBLISHERS, INC.

Published in the United States of America
by Rowman & Littlefield Publishers, Inc.
An imprint of the Rowman & Littlefield Publishing Group, Inc.
4501 Forbes Boulevard, Suite 200, Lanham, Maryland 20706

PO Box 317
Oxford
OX2 9RU, UK

British Library Cataloguing in Publication Information Available

Library of Congress Cataloging-in-Publication Data

Simon, Rita James.
   Global Perspectives on Social Issues: Education / Rita J. Simon and
Lisa Banks.
     p. cm.
Includes bibliographical references and index.
   ISBN 0-7391-0675-9 (hardcover : alk. paper)
  1. Comparative education. 2. Education—Cross-cultural studies. 3.
Education—Social aspects—Cross-cultural studies. I. Banks, Lisa,
1968– II. Title.
   LB43.S53 2003
370'.9—dc21
                                                2003011838

∞™ The paper used in this publication meets the minimum requirements of American
National Standard for Information Sciences—Permanence of Paper for Printed Library
Materials, ANSI/NISO Z39.48-1992.

Contents

Figures

Tables

1

Introduction

Global Perspectives on Social Issues: Education offers a broad perspective on education in twenty different nations. It provides an international context for examining and comparing the condition of education in various countries around the world. Each nation is presented within its own cultural context in order to reflect their social and political differences. The countries are grouped into eight different regions: North America, Latin America, Western Europe, Eastern Europe, Africa, the Middle East, Asia, and Oceania. The countries included in this study are: the United States, Canada, Brazil, Argentina, Great Britain, Italy, Germany, Spain, the Russian Federation, Poland, South Africa, Nigeria, Iraq, Egypt, Israel, India, China, Japan, New Zealand, and Australia.

Highlighted in this study are the basic components of each country's educational system—including literacy and enrollment rates, government expenditures on education, financing of education, and the presence and role of private schools. The aim at each level of the educational system is identified: pre-primary, compulsory, post-compulsory, technical and vocational, and adult education, along with current reform ideas for the existing system. These components are set within each country's demographic and social structures, which is intended to aid the reader in making inferences about the reasons behind the countries' varied educational systems.

2

Overview

Education is the key to the success of any nation; it is essential for evolutionary progress in technology and industrialization, as well as civic and cultural advancement. One of the first acts of any nation that launches a program of development is usually to initiate or expand its universities and other institutions of post-secondary education.[1] Results of the 1999 UNICEF Report on Education found that education is the single most important element in combating poverty, empowering women, safeguarding children from exploitation, promoting human rights and democracy, protecting the environment, and fostering international peace and security.

Nicholas J. Haiducek, the former director of education at Tokyo American College in Japan, predicted in the 1980s that by the twenty-first century, the success of a nation would be measured by its ability to educate its citizens. Today, students throughout the world who are finishing their education are entering a workforce that is part of a global economy. For a country to be competitive, the skills of its graduates must be equal to those of graduates from school systems around the world.[2] Recently, countries throughout the world have been investing a significant amount of time and resources into their education systems. Almost 20 percent of all people in the world are directly involved in education as either students or teachers in elementary schools, high schools, colleges, or universities. In industrialized countries such as the United States, Japan, and Canada, about 25 percent of people are directly involved in education.

Every nation has its own political and cultural ideology, which strongly influences its education system. In Russia, for example, the aftermath of communism is still evident in its educational system. Schools in South Africa are still struggling to abolish apartheid. In India, the centuries-old customs of the caste system are still prevalent. Religion also substantially influences the educational systems in many countries. The Israeli educational system, for example, is derived from both Jewish tradition and modern history. Currently, Israel is trying to temper the bond between religion and education but religion remains a strong influence on its educational system.

In addition, a country's legal framework largely determines how education will be administered. For example, the Indian Constitution grants women equal rights, but strong patriarchal traditions persist, and women's lives continue to be shaped by centuries-old customs and distinctions based on caste, class, ethnicity, and religion. In most Indian families a daughter is viewed as a burden and a disappointment. From early childhood, girls are usually conditioned to believe that they are inferior and subordinate to men. Thus, many parents, especially those in rural areas, feel that there is no point in educating their daughters, since they will soon be married off and will live with their in-laws.[3]

More recently, many nations of the world have recognized education as one of the most important human rights. Moving toward a quality educational system is therefore among the chief policy concerns internationally, and governments and educational organizations worldwide are striving to increase the quality, standards, goals, and accessibility of education.

In many underdeveloped nations, a lack of supplies inhibits the basic education of citizens. In Nigeria, for example, classroom space is inadequate and many students are either instructed in open-air or shared classrooms with up to four other grade levels. They have an inadequate supply of materials. Schools lack offices, desks, and other facilities, and have few or no toilets. Poor working conditions, extremely low remuneration, and inadequate facilities have eroded motivation and satisfaction.[4]

Latin American countries, on the other hand, have made major advancements in improving the quality of education. They have extended the years of compulsory education, provided early and preschool educa-

tion, access for the disabled, and improved access to education for indigenous children. Yet, economic conditions still continue to be a critical
issue, as the educational system continues to be segregated by class, with
the poor attending public schools and the middle and upper classes attending private institutions.[5]

Despite the vast differences in the quality of education worldwide,
most nations divide education into similar stages. Thus, formal education in many nations begins with pre-primary education and continues
through elementary, secondary, and higher education. Most school systems in all modern nations provide both general education and vocational education. Many countries provide special education programs for
disabled or gifted children. Adult education programs are another option
provided for people who wish to continue their education.

All countries represented in this study have a mandatory time period
during which children are required to attend school. The purpose of
compulsory education is to provide every child with a basic education.
More years of compulsory education often correspond to a higher education level in a given country. (See table A.3 in the appendix.) But
attendance is not always possible due to external factors such as a shortage of teachers or schools, distance from schools, and the economic
conditions in a family.

In many countries, a vast majority of children only receive an elementary education. Secondary and higher education are available only to
gifted students or to those who can afford to attend private institutions.
These nations include most developing countries and some Eastern European countries.

Unlike school districts in the United States, the school systems of most
other countries provide more than one kind of secondary education. For
example, students in most European countries may attend a general
school, which specializes in academic subjects, or they may attend a vocational school. Some of the vocational schools prepare students for advanced vocational or technical training. Others train students to enter
business or a trade immediately after they graduate.

In many countries, students are required to take an examination to determine what kind of secondary school they will attend. Some students
are admitted to academic schools, which prepare them for advanced
studies in a university. Other students are admitted to vocational schools.
Some countries with two or more forms of secondary education are

changing the system to include both general and vocational studies in the school curricula.

The United States has more students who receive a college education than most other countries. (See table A.7 in the appendix.) A few extremely poor nations do not have a single college or university, although most countries have at least one institution of higher learning.

The importance of education worldwide cannot be overestimated. According to a UNICEF 1998 publication, "Nearly a billion people will enter the twenty-first century unable to read a book or sign their names, two-thirds are women." A 1989 UNICEF report stated: "If the enhancement of people's capacity to improve their own lives is the main aim and measure of development, then nothing could contribute more directly to its achievement than education and literacy" (cited by Grant, 1989, pp. 51–52).

As education is recognized around the globe as essential to a country's development, literacy is no longer defined simply in terms of reading ability. Rather, literacy is now equated with an individual's ability to use written information to function effectively in society. Unlike generations ago, adults need a higher level of literacy to function effectively in modern society. Illiteracy may have serious implications, even threatening a nation's economic strength and social cohesion.[6] When considering literacy rates, it is helpful to view males and females separately. In some countries, especially in rural or poor communities, more than half the female population aged fifteen and over can neither read nor write. (See figure A.2 in the appendix.) While literacy rates are climbing worldwide, there are still tremendous differences among regions of the world. Literacy also varies within a country's own borders. In India, for example, the overall literacy rate for both men and women is 56 percent, but in some rural areas it drops to 50 percent. (See table A.1 in the appendix.) Generally, literacy is highest among whites in metropolitan centers and lowest among people of color in rural areas.

School enrollment rates are helpful indicators of the emphasis a country places on education. It is also an indicator of a country's educational and social trends and its commitment to higher education. Pre-primary education in all twenty countries studied is not compulsory. But over 90 percent of children four and older are enrolled in school in Spain, Italy, and England. In Italy, the rate for three-year-olds in pre-primary education is over 90 percent.

Worldwide, girls are still outnumbered by boys in primary and secondary school. (See tables A.5, A.6, and A.7 in the appendix.) Yet girls' enrollment is rising steadily, although slowly, and over the past two decades the gap in enrollment has been cut by more than 50 percent. In higher education in more than forty countries, women students outnumber men and more and more women are enrolling in traditionally male-dominated courses. Vocational and technical schools as well as adult education courses are becoming more widespread with the awareness of the benefits of continuing education.

Most countries have an educational system that is completely or partly administered by the central government, which exercises a high degree of control over certain aspects of the educational system. These countries often have ministries of education, which decide educational policy. The majority of countries have both public and private schools. In most countries, the majority of elementary and secondary school-aged children attend public schools.

Government expenditure on education as a share of gross national product varies from country to country. (See figure A.3 in the appendix.) For the most part, those countries that spend more on education tend to place a greater importance on education. Rates vary from 8 percent in South Africa to 2.3 percent in China. Public expenditures for education as a percentage of the gross domestic product also vary widely across the nations of the world. (See table A.2 in the appendix.)

In every nation, public education is supported mainly by public funds. Most countries that permit private schools also provide some financial support for such schools. Nations provide public funds for education in various ways. In most countries, including the most heavily populated countries, the national government shares the cost of education with other levels of government, such as states, provinces, or cities. In many of these countries, the national government supplies most of the funds. In other countries, including China and India, the funds come mainly from lower levels of government. In other countries, the national government pays all public education costs.[7]

Many countries obtain additional funds for public education from tuition fees, voluntary contributions, and other private sources. Some developing nations may receive foreign aid for education. For private schools, fellowships, grants, and financial aid are available. Compulsory public education is free throughout the world but some nations provide free education at every level. In the United Kingdom, for example, students have all their educational and living expenses paid until they have completed secondary school. But only highly gifted students receive this privilege. Egypt recently enacted a law making education free up to the doctoral level; since that time enrollment has increased tremendously in all higher education institutions. The Egyptian government also guarantees employment for all college graduates who cannot locate acceptable private sector employment within one year after graduation.

Enrollment rates, literacy rates, and years of compulsory education can say a great deal about the importance a country places on education. It is necessary when evaluating educational systems to look past these trends and evaluate the system as related to their own historical, cultural, and political background. As we entered the twenty-first century, the importance of education has increasingly influenced human rights issues, because it is through education that we can most easily combat ignorance and poverty. Education is a strong and vital force for social change. As the Convention on the Rights of the Child states: "Education is the foundation of a free and fulfilled life. It is the right of all children and the obligation of all governments."[8]

Notes

1. Patrick Uchendu, *Politics and Education in Nigeria* (Enugu, Nigeria: Fourth Dimension, 1995).

2. Roy Pearson, Erica O'Neal, Laura Saganik, and Marilyn McMillen, *Public Attitudes Toward Secondary Education: The United States in an International Context* NCES 97–595 (Washington, D.C.: U.S. Department of Education, National Center for Education Statistics, 1997).

3. Naomi Neft and Ann D. Levine, *Where Women Stand: An International Report on the Status of Women in 140 Countries, 1997–1998* (New York: Random House, 1997), 296.

4. Paul A. Francis, *Hard Lessons: Primary Schools, Community and Social Capital in Nigeria* (Washington, D.C.: World Bank, 1998), xiii.

5. Ernesto Schifelbein, "Financing Education for Democracy in Latin America," in Carlos Alberto Torres and Adriana Puiggros, eds., *Latin American Education Comparative Perspectives* (Boulder, Colo.: Westview Press, 1997).

6. T. Scott Murray, Irwin S. Kirsh, and Lynn B. Jenkins; Project Officer, Marilyn Binkley, *Adult Literacy in OCED Countries: Technical Report on the First International Adult Literacy Survey,* NCFS 98–053 (Washington, D.C.: U.S. Department of Education, National Center for Education Statistics, 1998), 13.

7. *World Book Encyclopedia,* 83rd ed., s.v. "education."

8. UNICEF, "Introduction," in *State of the World's Children 1999* (New York: Oxford University Press for UNICEF, 1999).

3

Country Profiles: North America

UNITED STATES

Background Information

The United States occupies a large portion of North America, stretching across the continent between Mexico and Canada, and includes Hawaii in the Pacific Ocean and Alaska on the northwestern border of Canada. With 263.4 million people, the United States is the third-largest nation in the world in population, behind only China and India. In area, it is the fourth-largest country after Russia, Canada, and China.

Three-fourths of the U.S. population live in urban areas, and more than forty metropolitan areas have populations over 1 million. Approximately 83 percent of Americans are Caucasian, 12.5 percent are African American, 4 percent are Asian or Pacific Islander, and 0.8 percent are American Indian, Eskimo, or Aleut. Hispanic Americans make up 10 percent of the population.

The United States is a democratic nation headed by a president who holds executive power. The Congress, consisting of the House of Representatives and the Senate, exercises legislative power. The judicial power rests in the hands of the Supreme Court, which interprets the highest law of the land, the Constitution.

For administrative purposes the country is divided into fifty territories known as states, and the District of Columbia, the nation's capital. Each state has its own executive, legislative, and judicial powers. Each state is also subject to the laws made by the federal government, which surpasses any state law.

English is the official language and is the language of instruction for educational purposes and on official documents.

There is no established religion in the United States. Under the Constitution, individuals have the freedom to practice whichever religion they choose. Fifty-six percent of Americans are Protestant, 26 percent are Roman Catholic, and 2 percent are Jewish. There are many other religions represented in smaller minorities, such as Muslims, Hindus, and Buddhists.

Basis of the Educational System—Principles and Legislation

The Constitution of the United States makes no reference to education. But the Tenth Amendment to the Constitution gives the states any powers the Constitution does not prohibit or specifically grant to the federal government. Because the Constitution does not give the federal government control over education, the states assume this responsibility. But the Constitution gives Congress the power to provide for the "general welfare of the United States"[1] and the Congress has used this power to deal with educational matters that affect many Americans. (See table 3.1.)

Control of the Educational System

All fifty states have laws governing education and have an established system of public schools. A state school system provides for every level of education, from early childhood through higher education. Every state except Hawaii has transferred some of its control over public education to local school districts. According to federal regulations agreed to by the states, school districts are responsible for running the local public schools, hiring teachers, constructing buildings, and planning the curriculum. Each state government determines the number and organization of school districts in the state.[2]

TABLE 3.1
Important Dates in U.S. Education

1635	The Boston Latin School, the first secondary school in the American Colonies, began classes.
1636	Massachusetts chartered Harvard College, the first college in the American Colonies.
1642	Massachusetts passed an education law requiring parents to teach their children to read.
1647	Massachusetts became the first American colony to require establishment of public elementary and secondary education.
1785	Georgia chartered the first state university.
1795	The University of North Carolina became the first state university to hold classes.
1819	The U.S. Supreme Court ruled that a state cannot take over a private college without its permission.
1833	Oberlin Collegiate Institute (now Oberlin College) became the first coeducational college in the United States.
1852	Massachusetts passed the first compulsory school attendance law in the United States.
1862	The Morrill Act gave federal land to support state agricultural and technical colleges.
1874	The Michigan Supreme Court ruled that taxes could be collected to support public high schools.
1917	Congress passed the Smith-Hughes Act, the first act to provide federal funds for vocational education below the college level.
1944	Congress passed the first GI Bill, granting funds to veterans to continue their education.
1954	The U.S. Supreme Court ruled that public schools segregated by race are unequal and therefore unconstitutional.
1965	Congress passed the Elementary and Secondary Education Act to aid local schools to improve the education of children from low-income families.
1972	Congress passed the Education Amendments Act, which grants funds to almost every institution of higher learning to use as it wishes.
1978	The U.S. Supreme Court ruled that college and university admission programs may not use specific quotas to achieve racial balance. But they may give special consideration to members of minority groups.
1979	Congress established the U.S. Department of Education.
1983	The National Commission on Excellence in Education reported in *A Nation at Risk* that U.S. students lagged far behind students in many other industrialized nations.
1994	Michigan became the first state to sharply reduce the use of property taxes in the financing of its public schools.

Almost every state has an elected or appointed board of education and an elected or appointed superintendent or commissioner of education. Most states also have a department of education at the state level, which is composed of the state educational agencies. The state's board of education sets state educational policies. The state superintendent, who heads the department of education, sees that the board's policies are carried out. Hawaii is the only state in which the state superintendent and department of education directly control the local public schools.[3]

Certain private organizations have indirect control over education. For example, the National Education Association of the United States (NEA), a large organization of teachers and school administrators, uses its influence to improve the quality of schools and teaching. Many private foundations also influence education, such as the Ford Foundation and the Carnegie Corporation of New York, by granting money for scholarships and research programs.[4]

The federal Department of Education is an executive department of the U.S. government; the Department's fundamental goal is to improve education at all levels. It also promotes equal educational opportunities for all citizens. The Department's responsibilities fall into six main categories:

1. providing leadership in addressing critical issues in American education;
2. assisting in the collection of ideas for the improvement of education;
3. helping students pay for their education beyond high school;
4. helping communities and schools meet the needs of their students;
5. preparing students for employment; and
6. working to ensure equal educational opportunities for all Americans.[5]

The Organization of the Educational System

Formal education in the United States is divided into three stages or levels that follow one another: elementary, secondary and post-secondary education. Students typically spend from six to eight years in the elementary grades, which may be preceded by one to two years in nursery school and kindergarten. A four- to six-year program in secondary school follows the elementary school program. Students usually complete secondary school, through grade twelve, by age seventeen or eighteen.

High school graduates who decide to continue their education may enter a technical or vocational institution, a two-year college, or a four-year college or university. A two-year college normally offers the first two years of a four-year college curriculum and contains various vocational programs. Most academic courses completed in a two-year college are transferable to a four-year university or college. A technical or vocational institution offers post-secondary technical training targeted at a specific career.

An associate's degree requires at least two years of college level work, and a bachelor's degree can normally be earned in four years. At least one year beyond the bachelor's is necessary for a master's degree, while a doctorate degree requires a minimum of three or four years beyond the bachelor's degree.

Professional schools differ widely in admission requirements and length of study. Medical students, for example, generally complete a four-year program of premedical study at a college or university before entering a four-year program at a medical school. A law degree normally requires three years of study beyond the bachelor's degree level.[6]

Pre-primary Education

Pre-primary education represents the initial stage of the educational system. It is also referred to as preschool or kindergarten and is generally designed for children five years of age and younger. Its primary objective is to develop habits and skills that will better prepare students for learning experiences that follow in elementary education. According to recent studies, children who attend preschool are more likely to perform better than those who do not. In the United States, about half of all children ages three through five attend some kind of preschool or kindergarten.

Compulsory Education

Education in all fifty states is compulsory for children from age six or seven until the age of sixteen.

Elementary Education

Elementary education begins at the age of about six or seven and continues until age twelve or fourteen. Elementary schools are also called grammar schools. A traditional elementary school is divided into six or eight grades. Students in each grade level must meet set standards before they can advance to the next grade.

Most students enter a secondary school after completing elementary education. But many school systems have established "middle schools" for pupils of upper-elementary school age—that is from age ten to twelve to about fourteen. Most middle schools contain grades six through eight, but some include grade five. Elementary schools are designed to develop skills that will better prepare a student for more advanced studies.

Secondary Education

Secondary schooling in the United States refers to high schools. High schools are designed to help students become responsible members of the community and to prepare them for a job or for higher education. Upon completion of high school, students receive a diploma that verifies that they have completed their secondary education. Almost all school-aged children in the United States enroll in high school, and most students graduate.

Most communities have four-year high schools consisting of grades nine through twelve. These schools enroll graduates of eight-year elementary schools, junior high schools, or middle schools. Other communities have separate junior and senior high schools. Most junior high schools include grades seven through nine. Most students enter junior high school after attending a six-year elementary school. They continue their education and prepare for senior high school. Most junior high school graduates attend a three-year senior high school, which consists of grades ten through twelve. Some communities combine junior and senior high school.

Most high schools offer both general and vocational courses of study. Most often these schools are called comprehensive high schools. Students who wish to continue on to higher education will take a general, college preparatory course of study. Often, if a student intends to work after graduation, a vocational course of study may be a more practical option.

Post-secondary Education

American colleges and universities offer diverse educational experiences at the post-secondary level. More than half of all high school graduates continue on to pursue some form of higher education. The United States has thousands of different institutions of higher learning. Over half are privately owned and operated; most of these are small liberal arts colleges. Many are large, publicly-owned state universities. About four-fifths of all the college and university students in the United States attend public institutions.

Post-secondary education includes various educational institutions, such as community and junior colleges, technical institutions, colleges, universities, and professional schools. Community and junior colleges offer two-year programs in both general and career education. Most technical schools offer two-year programs in such fields as automotive engineering, business, and electronics. After completing courses at a two-year community college, junior college, or technical institute, a student receives an associate's degree, or a certificate in the case of certain types of specialized training. Colleges and universities provide a wide selection of liberal arts career programs. Most offer a four- or five-year liberal arts program leading to a bachelor's degree.

Many colleges and most universities offer advanced courses leading to a masters or doctoral degree. Most universities also have professional schools, which provide training and award degrees in such areas as business, dentistry, education, engineering, law, and medicine. Students often complete a certain amount of college-level course work before entering professional schools.

Private Schools

Parents in the United States have the option of sending their children to public schools, or they may enroll them in private schools that are independent of state control. Most private schools are controlled by religious organizations. Private schools controlled by religious groups are called parochial schools. The Roman Catholic Church controls most of the parochial schools in the United States. While public education is free, private schooling is funded and operated by tuition fees. Fees for private schooling vary according to the institution. Private schools are available to students from the preschool level through higher and adult education.

Financing Education

Funding for public education comes almost entirely from local, state, and federal taxes. Private schools are supported mainly by tuition fees and by contributions from churches, private organizations, wealthy benefactors, and former students. In recent years, the cost for education in both public and private institutions has gone up dramatically, due in part to increases in population and the demand for higher salaries for teachers. As a result, most school districts need more money than taxes provide.

State school districts pay almost half of the total costs of public elementary and secondary education. In most districts, federal tax dollars pay only a small percentage of school funding costs. Many districts are facing serious financial difficulties. As a result, many school systems have been forced to reduce and eliminate many of their educational programs.

Private schools also have been faced with financial problems. As part of a 2002 decision upholding school vouchers, the Supreme Court ruled that public funds may be used by parents to pay tuition at parochial schools. In some instances, private schools may receive certain benefits such as textbooks and transportation. Private colleges and universities receive relatively large sums of money from the federal government. (See figure 3.1.)

Various agencies and branches of the federal government are responsible for allocating funds, regulating programs approved by Congress, and dealing with other educational matters. Congress decides how much money the government will spend on education and what types of educational programs federal funds will support. The Supreme Court and other federal courts have the authority to decide constitutional questions relating to education.

The government spends billions of dollars on education annually. (See figure 3.2.) Some of the money supports educational institutions owned

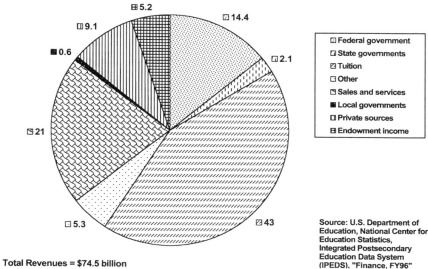

Total Revenues = $74.5 billion

Source: U.S. Department of Education, National Center for Education Statistics, Integrated Postsecondary Education Data System (IPEDS), "Finance, FY96"

FIGURE 3.1
Sources of Current Fund Revenue for Private Institutions: 1995–1996

and operated by the federal government. The largest federal educational expenditures are for higher education and for certain educational programs administered by the states.

The federal government gives significant sums of money to individual state departments of education. But Congress distributes most of the

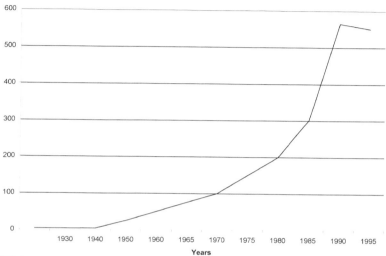

FIGURE 3.2
Annual Expenditures for U.S. Education

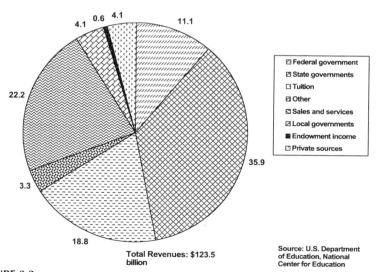

Legend:
- Federal government
- State governments
- Tuition
- Other
- Sales and services
- Local governments
- Endowment income
- Private sources

Total Revenues: $123.5 billion

Source: U.S. Department of Education, National Center for Education

FIGURE 3.3
Sources of Current Fund Revenue for Public Institutions of Higher Education: 1995–1996

funds among local school districts, which may use them for specified purposes. For example, Congress grants large sums of money to local districts to provide special services for children from low-income families. Local districts receive federal money for textbooks, to pay for school health facilities, and to finance experimental educational programs.

The federal government pays about 13 percent of the total costs of higher education in the United States. The government grants loans and scholarships to college and university students to help pay for their tuition and other school expenses. The government also grants funds to public and private institutions of higher education. Without federal aid many colleges and universities would be forced to close.[7]

Adult Education

Millions of adults in the United States participate in some form of adult education. A number of colleges and universities provide extension courses which grant adults the opportunity to take classes at the college level. Many of these classes are scheduled for the evening hours so that students can attend after work. Businesses, community agencies, correspondence schools, hospitals, industries, labor unions, prisons, libraries, museums, and television stations provide various organized educational opportunities for adults. Courseloads range from elementary English and arithmetic to advanced commercial, technical and professional training.

Alternative Forms of Education

Various courts in the United States have held that parents may educate their children at home. If educated at home, however, the children must receive an education equal to that of the public school. States often test children educated outside the public school system to ensure that they meet standards set for students who attend public schools.

Literacy Rates

Literacy rates in the United States are among the highest in the world at 99 percent for both men and women. (See table A.1 in the appendix.) While literacy rates are high, functional illiteracy (i.e., the inability to read or write well enough to function in society) is estimated to affect one-fifth of all adults in the United States. The Department of Education has established various programs throughout the country to help eradicate illiteracy. For example, some school districts have established adult reading centers to teach illiterate parents how to read and educate their children.

School Enrollment Rates

In the fall of 1999, about 68.1 million persons were enrolled in American schools and colleges. While attendance rates vary, it is accurate to say that most children attend school in the United States. Pre-primary school is not compulsory. But about half of all children ages three through five attend some kind of preschool or kindergarten classes. Enrollment in public elementary and secondary schools rose to 45.5 million in 1999. Private school enrollment grew more slowly than public school enrollment, rising 7 percent from 5.6 million in 1985 to 6.0 million in 1999. College enrollment hit a record level of 14.2 million in the fall of 1996 and was expected to reach a new high of 14.9 million in 1999. (See table 3.2 and figure 3.4; see also tables A.5, A.6, and A.7 in the appendix.)

TABLE 3.2
School Enrollment Rates among Primary, Secondary, and Tertiary Schools

	Country	Primary	Secondary	Tertiary
1	United States	24,045,967	21,473,692	14,261,778
2	Canada	2, 448,144	2,505,389	1,763,105
3	Brazil	35,838,372	6,967,905	1,868,529
4	Argentina	5,153,256	2,594,329	
5	United Kingdom	5,284,125	6,548,786	1,820,849
6	Italy	2,816,128	4,602,243	1,892,542
7	Germany	3,804,887	8,382,335	2,131,907
8	Spain	2,567,012	3,852,102	1,684,445
9	Russia	7,849,000		
10	Poland	5,021,378	2,539,138	720,267
11	South Africa	8,159,430		
12	Nigeria	16,190,947		
13	Iraq	2,903,923	1,160,421	197,800
14	Egypt	7,499,303	6,726,738	
15	Israel	631,916	541,737	198,766
16	Japan	7,855,387		
17	China	139,954,000	71,883,000	6,075,215
18	India	110,390,406	68,872,393	6,060,418
19	New Zealand	357,569	433,347	169,656
20	Australia	1,855,789	2,367,692	1,041,648

*Statistics from United Nations Education, Scientific and Cultural Organization (UNESCO)

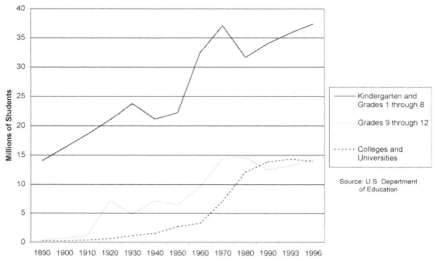

FIGURE 3.4
School Enrollment in the United States

Reforms in Current Educational System

Teachers, students, parents, and policy makers continually debate many issues involving education. Some controversial areas of debate include the curriculum in schools across the country, how performance in various subjects should be measured and improved, the type of school children should attend, who should teach, who should be educated, how schools should be managed, and how education should be financed. It is these issues that educators, policy makers, and parents are seeking to address in efforts to make education more equal, thereby ensuring that all Americans receive not only an education but a quality education.

Notes

1. Constitution of the United States of America.
2. *World Book Encyclopedia*, 83rd ed., s.v. "education."
3. Ibid.
4. Ibid.

5. *World Book Encyclopedia*, 83rd ed., s.v. "department of education."

6. Thomas Snyder, Charlene M. Hoffman, production manager, *Digest of Educational Statistics, 1999* NCES 200–031 (Washington, D.C.: U.S. Department of Education, National Center for Educational Statistics, 2000), 5.

7. *World Book Encyclopedia*, 83rd ed., s.v. "education."

CANADA

Background Information

Canada occupies most of the northern portion of North America. It is bordered on the north by the Arctic Ocean, on the northeast by the Baffin Bay and Davis Strait, on the east by the Atlantic Ocean, on the south by the United States, and on the west by Alaska and the Pacific Ocean.

In area, Canada is the second largest country in the world, behind only Russia. But its population is relatively small at 28.5 million. Canada has approximately the same population as the state of California, which is one-twenty-fifth its size.

For administrative purposes, Canada is divided into a federation of ten provinces—Alberta, British Columbia, Manitoba, New Brunswick, Newfoundland, Nova Scotia, Ontario, Prince Edward Island, Quebec, and Saskatchewan—and three territories, the Northwest, Yukon, and Nunavut Territories. The governor general, who has no political power, heads the country. The chief executive is the Prime Minister, who answers to a legislature. The Canadian Parliament answers to its citizens. The federal and provincial governments appoint judges.

Most Canadians live in the Southern portions of the country. About 77 percent of Canadians inhabit urban areas and more than half the population live in two provinces, Ontario and Quebec.

Canada is officially a bilingual country, and all services provided by the federal government are available in English and French. The most prevalent nonofficial languages are, in order of prominence: Chinese, Italian, Punjabi, Spanish, Portuguese, and Polish.

French is taught to students in Quebec unless certain conditions apply, such as if the child's parents were taught in an English-language school. While there are a few exceptions, English is the principal language of instruction in provinces other than Quebec and in the territories. Many New Brunswick schools, for example, are French-language schools. French immersion programs are also popular within Canada where students are taught almost completely in French.

Most Canadians are Christian, although a growing number of Canadians claim no religious affiliation. Approximately 46 percent are Roman Catholic, most others are Protestant. A small percentage of Canadians are Jews, Muslims, and more recently Buddhists, Hindus, and Sikhs.

Basis of Educational System—Principles and Legislation

Canada's federal government has no constitutional authority in education and therefore maintains no central office dealing directly with educational matters. Nevertheless, federal activities related to education are carried out under other auspices. For example, certain functions are the responsibility of an office of education that is under the secretary of state. For the most part, individual provinces have a great deal of autonomy over education.

Control of the Educational System

Canada, like the United States, does not have a national education system. Instead each province and territory organizes and regulates its own system of education. While there are many similarities among educational structures and institutions across the country, each jurisdiction has developed a system that best reflects the historical and cultural heritage of its citizens.

Each province has a department of education headed by a minister of education. The department sets educational policies and standards for the entire province. A province is divided into local school districts, and each of these has a school board and a superintendent. Local school districts have a considerable amount of control over their institutions.

Although there is no national system of education, the federal government intervenes for special populations outside normal provincial jurisdiction, such as inmates of federal prisons, the families of Canadian armed forces, Inuits and Eskimos. To discuss universal issues of concern Canada established the Council of Ministers of Education, Canada (CMEC) in 1967. The CMEC is the national voice for education in Canada. It is the mechanism through which ministers consult and act on matters of mutual interest, and the instrument through which they consult and cooperate with national organizations and the federal government. CMEC also represents the interests of the provinces and territories internationally.[1]

Organization of the Educational System

Compulsory education in Canada begins at the age of six or seven and lasts until the age of sixteen. Most school districts offer education to students from kindergarten through twelfth grade. Students who plan to seek employment after completing compulsory education may take a two-year vocational course in high school. Students who plan to continue their education take a four- or five-year general course. Canada has about eighty degree-granting institutions that are members of the Association of Universities and Colleges of Canada. Other institutions of higher learning include technical institutions and community colleges. In Canada, a community college combines the last two years of high school and the first two years of college.

Pre-primary Education

Most jurisdictions offer preschool or kindergarten programs that are operated by the local education authorities. Children between the ages of three and five typically attend preschool. In such institutions, children learn basic personal skills and habits that will aid the child in adapting to society. Pre-primary education also prepares young children for their more advanced education.

Compulsory Education

The Canadian education system requires a minimum of ten years of schooling for all children. The ages for compulsory education vary from one jurisdiction to another, but generally, schooling is obligatory from ages six to sixteen. (See table A.3 in the appendix.)

Elementary and Secondary Education

Elementary schools in most jurisdictions cover the first six to eight years of compulsory education. Afterward, children proceed to a secondary education program. A great variety of programs, vocational as well as academic, are offered at the secondary level. Secondary school diplomas are granted to students who pass the compulsory and optional courses in their programs.[2]

The point of transition from elementary to secondary school may vary from jurisdiction to jurisdiction. The elementary–secondary continuum can be broken up into different grade combinations. In many northern and rural communities, schools offer all grade levels, kindergarten to twelfth grade. In Quebec, secondary schooling ends after eleven years of study. In Ontario, students usually complete the secondary school diploma requirements, including Ontario Academic Courses, in four to five years. But in

Ontario, students who entered the ninth grade in 1999 were required to follow a new four-year program.[3]

Post-secondary Education

Universities are still the dominant institutions offering higher education, but the number of non-university post-secondary institutions, particularly community colleges, has increased in recent decades.

At a university, it is possible to study at three different levels, leading to bachelors, masters, or doctoral degrees. In addition to degree programs, most universities offer diploma and certificate programs. These programs can be either at the undergraduate or graduate level, and can range from one to three years. Most Canadian universities, especially the larger ones, offer a complete range of programs. But not all universities offer graduate programs.

Enrollment in trade–vocational programs such as apprenticeships or other programs geared towards preparation for employment in an occupation or trade generally do not require graduation from secondary school. Not all students who attend post-secondary institutions do so directly from high school. For example, a student may enter a college program after obtaining a university degree. Post-secondary education is available in the government-supported and private institutions, some of which award degrees.

In general, colleges award only diplomas or certificates; they do not award degrees. But the university transfer programs in the community college system in Alberta and British Columbia, and to a lesser extent Manitoba and the Northwest Territories, allows students to complete two years of academic course work toward bachelors degrees. These programs allow students to complete the third or fourth years at a university college or university, and receive a degree. In many provinces and territories, students must apply for admission and have their college studies evaluated before being granted credit for completed courses.[4]

Private Schools

Most private schools charge tuition fees. Private schooling is available at every level of education in the Canadian school system. Churches frequently play an essential role in education. Church-run schools are the most common alternative to the secular system of education and exist in all provinces and territories. Typically these church-run schools receive state funding if they agree to teach the standard curriculum, as well as the extra language courses and/or religion courses. Many Roman Catholic schools, especially in Quebec, teach in French. Most Protestant and non-religious schools teach in English.[5]

Financing Education

Public education is provided free of charge to all Canadian citizens and permanent residents until the end of secondary school, concluding normally at the age of eighteen. Canada's investment in education is among the highest in the world, as measured by OCED indicators of education expenditure. In 1995, Canada had the highest expenditure on education as a proportion of gross domestic product among G7 countries, and the second highest per student expenditure. (See table 3.3.)

Canadian educators are increasingly occupied with the issue of funding current education programs while budgets are shrinking. In 1997, all governments combined spent C$51.7 billion on education, which was six percent of Canada's gross domestic product. Almost all provincial governments have adopted deficit reduction strategies that have made allocating funds for schools difficult.

Canada's provincial governments share the cost of public education with the local school districts. In six provinces, Alberta, British Columbia, Newfoundland, Ontario, Quebec, and Saskatchewan, public funds are also used to support religious schools. The other provinces provide little or no aid to religious schools. (See table 3.4.)

TABLE 3.3
Expenditures on Education, by Education Level: 1995–1996

	Canada	Newfoundland	Prince Edward Island	Nova Scotia	New Brunswick
			$ millions		
Education expenditures*	58,943.71	1,360.70	228.79	1,627.53	1,363.10
Level					
Elementary and secondary	36,424.71	584.33	120.88	919.45	819.39
Community college	4,531.82	40.76	12.95	48.23	58.51
University	11,801.98	239.88	41.81	441.38	302.72
Vocational training	6,185.20	495.73	53.15	218.48	182.49

Continued

TABLE 3.3 *Continued*

Direct source of funds					
Federal government**	5,754.13	503.43	58.54	283.59	213.18
Provincial governments	32,179.93	757.82	157.04	1,006.73	1,042.14
Municipal governments***	12,779.83	a	b	138.13	0.21
Fees and other sources	7,238.81	419.36	13.30	976.30	107.58

a amount too small to be expressed
b nil or zero
* Includes operating capital, student aid, and all departmental expenditures
** In addition to the direct funding reported here, the federal government also provides indirect support in respect of post-secondary education to provinces and territories under the Federal-Provincial Fiscal Arrangements and Federal Post-secondary Education and Health Contributions Act, 1977 and under the Official Languages in Education Program
*** Includes local school taxation

Source: Statistics Canada, CANSIM, Cross-classified tables 00590203, 00590204, 00590206, 00590305, 00590306, 00590206

The federal and provincial governments fund education at the university level in Canada, requiring students to pay only a small portion of the total cost. As public funding for post-secondary education fell during the 1990s, educational institutions increased tuition fees. For example, average tuition fees for undergraduate liberal arts programs more than doubled from $1,568 in 1988–1989 to $3,199 in 1998–1999.

TABLE 3.4
Direct Sources of Funds for Education at All Levels

	1993–1994	1994–1995	1995–1996	1996–1997	1997–1998*
	$ Millions				
All Funds	57,056.30	58,560.00	58,943.70	58,125.10	59,709.90
Government					
Federal**	6,288.00	6,630.30	6,754.10	6,006.50	6,663.00
Provincial	32,512.50	32,731.10	32,179.90	31,445.80	32,017.20
Municipal***	11,966.20	12,381.50	12,779.80	12,954.80	12,825.60
Fees	3,348.40	3,581.20	3,804.30	4,093.00	4,412.30
Other sources	2,941.10	3,235.90	3,434.50	3,625.10	3,791.70

* Preliminary data
** In addition to the direct funding reported here, the federal government also provides indirect support in respect of post-secondary education to provinces and territories under the Federal-Provincial Fiscal Arrangements and Federal Post-secondary Education and Health Contributions Act, 1977 and under the Official Languages in Education Program
*** Includes local school taxation

Source: Statistics Canada, CANSIM, Cross-classified tables 00590203, 00590204, 00590206, 00590306

Community college tuition remains lower than university tuition in most programs.

In recent years, the government has offered special scholarships to indigenous persons who wish to pursue full-time or part-time secondary education. Approximately two-thirds of the students who have accepted this offer have been women.

Adult Education

Adult education gives adults the opportunity to complete secondary school, pursue higher education, and/or expand employment training. Most colleges offer continuing education programs aimed at adults in the community and for developing skills for careers in business, the applied arts, technology, social services, and health sciences. The goals of these programs are to increase people's participation in society and in the workforce. Adult education and training also enhances Canada's international competitiveness by contributing to the development and maintenance of an educated, skilled and flexible work force. In 1997, approximately 27 percent of the population between the ages of twenty-five and fifty-four participated in specific job-related adult education and training.

Literacy Rates

Canada has among the highest literacy rates for both men and women at 99 percent. Complete illiteracy—the inability to read or write at all in any language—is rare in Canada. But there is a greater level of functional illiteracy—the inability to read well or to understand what is read. Illiteracy is more likely to be found among the old and the poor. Programs to combat illiteracy have been offered by the National Literacy Secretariat, which promotes and supports organizations dedicated to addressing adult illiteracy. (See table A.1 in the appendix.)

School Enrollment Rates

Participation in the school system is almost universal; in the 1993–1994 school year, 98.9 percent of all children of compulsory school

TABLE 3.5
Enrollment in Elementary and Secondary Schools

	Canada*	Public	Private	Federal	Visually and hearing impaired
1990-1991	5,141,003	4,845,308	240,968	52,285	2,442
1991-1992	5,218,237	4,915,630	245,255	55,221	2,131
1992-1993	5,284,145	4,967,848	257,605	56,416	2,276
1993-1994	5,327,826	5,002,834	265,275	57,378	2,339
1994-1995	5,362,799	5,029,114	271,974	59,383	2,328
1995-1996	5,430,836	5,085,386	278,721	64,268	2,461
1996-1997	5,414,555	5,065,914	279,969	66,327	2,345

* Canada total also includes Department of National Defence schools overseas

Source: Statistics Canada, Catalogue no. 81-229-X1B

age were enrolled in elementary and secondary schools. (See tables A.4, A.5, A.6, and A.7 in the appendix.) After the compulsory education is completed, participation decreases. Only 68.2 percent of all students graduate from secondary school. (See table 3.5.)

Although Canadian education levels are already high by international standards, they have continued to improve in recent years. More Canadians are graduating from high school and are pursuing higher education. Between 1990 and 1998, the percentage of twenty-five to twenty-nine-year-olds with less than high school education fell from 20 percent to 13 percent, while the percentage of university graduates increased from 17 percent to 26 percent. Many adults are participating in continuing education. In 1998, approximately 1.4 million Canadians adults aged twenty-five and over were enrolled in formal education programs. (See table 3.6.)

Women now comprise more than half of all college and university enrollments and graduates. In 1997, females received 58 percent of university diplomas and degrees, up from 53 percent a decade earlier. Women accounted for more than 80 percent of the increase in the number of university graduates over the ten-year period.

Reforms in the Current Educational System

Current reforms in the educational system of Canada have included programs to increase the standards and the quality of education. Canada has also put forth great efforts to eradicate illiteracy.

TABLE 3.6
University Enrollment, Full-Time and Part-Time

	1994-1995	1995-1996	1996-1997	1997-1998	1998-1999
			Both sexes		
Full-Time Enrollment					
Canada	575,713	573,194	573,635	573,099	580,376
Newfoundland	13,144	13,472	13,193	13,115	13,115
Pr. Edward Is.	2,544	2,425	2,313	2,452	2,470
Nova Scotia	29,922	29,723	29,941	30,077	30,027
New Brunswick	19,551	19,401	18,931	18,503	18,529
Quebec	135,603	132,927	132,054	131,074	134,162
Ontario	230,306	228,158	226,998	227,153	229,985
Manitoba	22,962	21,459	22,024	21,024	20,883
Saskatchewan	23,182	23,637	23,571	23,864	23,656
Alberta	50,803	52,399	53,044	52,824	53,510
Br. Columbia	47,696	49,593	51,566	53,013	54,039
Part-Time Enrollment					
Canada	283,257	273,215	256,133	249,673	245,985
Newfoundland	4,025	2,745	2,861	2,683	2,595
Pr. Edward Is.	587	476	424	482	417
Nova Scotia	7,323	6,917	6,894	7,006	7,214
New Brunswick	5,233	5,398	4,698	4,181	4,237
Quebec	112,818	109,106	103,639	101,021	98,116
Ontario	94,081	91,256	79,835	76,255	72,958
Manitoba	12,806	11,950	10,031	9,796	9,852
Saskatchewan	8,056	7,939	7,748	7,364	7,622
Alberta	16,632	15,519	16,990	18,594	20,263
Br. Columbia	21,687	21,909	23,013	22,291	22,711

Source: Statistics Canada, CANSIM, Cross-classified tables 00580701, 00580702

Notes

1. Council of Ministers of Education, Canada. <http://www.cmec.ca/indexe. stm>.
2. *Education Indicators in Canada; Report of the Pan-Canadian Education Indicators Program 1999.* (Toronto: Canadian Education Statistics Council, 2000), 133.
3. Ibid.
4. Ibid.
5. "Canada," *Microsoft Encarta Encyclopedia Standard 2001*, CD–ROM. (Redmond, Wash.: Microsoft Corporation, 2001).

Country Profiles: Latin America

BRAZIL

Background Information

Brazil is the most populous country and the largest country by area in South America. It extends from north of the equator to south of the Tropic of Capricorn.

Brazil's population is very diverse. This diversity stems from the mix of Native Americans, Africans, and Portuguese. Brazil is the only country in South America that is derived from the Portuguese tradition and heritage. Most Brazilians, 77 percent, live in cities.

Brazil has been a republic since 1889. Since its founding it has been under five different constitutions. The current constitution became effective in 1988. It created a republic with twenty-six federated states and one federal district. This constitution grants considerable powers to the legislative branch—the National Congress—to counter those of the president. It also shifted substantial responsibility and funding from the national government to the states and municipalities, which now have considerable autonomy over internal affairs. The current constitution also provides for the equality of all citizens under the law, and universal suffrage.

Brazil's government has three branches: a presidential branch, which exercises executive powers; a congressional branch, which consists of the Senate and Chamber of Deputies, and controls legislative power; and the Supreme Federal Tribunal, which heads the judicial branch of government. Portuguese is the official and primary language of Brazil, although there are some regional variations in pronunciation. Since 1938, Portuguese has been the official language for teaching in schools. German and Italian are still the most commonly spoken languages in homes in the south. English and French are the main second languages of educated Brazilians.

Roman Catholicism is the dominant religion in Brazil with 72 percent of the population claiming at least nominal affiliation. The church has played a major role in shaping many of the country's laws and policies, especially those concerning women. About 22 percent of Brazilians are members of Protestant churches. In recent years, Pentecostal groups have been growing rapidly.

Basis of the Educational System—Principles and Legislation

In 1971, Brazil instituted a major education reform that provided for basic compulsory education of eight years, with a universal curriculum. Students then may continue on to pursue training for employment or higher education. Despite provisions in the 1988 Constitution mandating federal expenditures for education, schooling remains under-funded and there are substantial variations that exist in opportunity between urban and rural children, and among social classes.[1]

The 1988 Brazilian Constitution established that education is a right of all people, and an obligation of the State and the family to provide. Education is intended to develop the individual and prepare them for citizenship and work. According to the Constitution, schooling should take into consideration equal access and continuity in the schools, freedom to learn, the pluralism of ideas, a free public school system, democratic practices, and standards of quality. Further, investment in education in Brazil is open to private investment as long as entrepreneurs abide by the general principles established by the Constitution.

The Constitution also features a provision to guarantee that indigenous communities maintain their language and their specific learning processes.[2] This constitutional right was intended to preserve and strengthen the indigenous peoples' social organization, cultures, customs, beliefs, and traditions. In 1996, Brazil had about 600 indigenous schools.

Control of the Educational System

The Union, or Central Government, the states, the federal district, and the municipalities are responsible for the organization of their respective educational systems in a regime of "collaboration."[3] The Union organizes and finances the federal system of education through technical and monetary assistance to the states and municipalities, which must provide for mandatory education.

The administration of education in Brazil involves federal, state, and municipal institutions. The state secretaries of education define their political and educational agendas through the Council of State Secretaries of Education and the municipal secretaries coordinate the Association of Leadership to Municipal Education. The Council of Rectors represents Brazilian universities. The federal Ministry of Education, as a part of the Executive branch, is responsible for enforcing all the educational laws and rules of the Federal Council on Education. The Federal Council on Education, in turn, has the role of handling education at the national level through the establishment of general educational guidelines and standards. The State Secretaries are responsible for coordinating educational policy at the state level and ensuring they are in compliance with State Councils of Education guidelines. The municipal secretaries of education coordinate activity and education within that jurisdiction.[4]

Private elementary and secondary education is subject to supervision by state agencies, and early childhood education is inspected by municipal administrations.

Organization of the Educational System

The National Education System includes public school systems and other public or private institutions, which deliver educational services. Its objective is to guarantee unity and cohesion among the various systems and ensure the same standard of quality throughout the national territory. The state system of education includes public and private schools as well as administrative, legislative, and technical support of state institutions.

The municipal system of education includes public and private schools, as in the case of the state system, and institutions and educational services within its jurisdiction.

Brazilian education is divided into two levels: basic and higher education. Basic Education includes early childhood education (ages one through six), elementary education (ages seven through fourteen), and secondary education (ages fifteen through seventeen).

Pre-primary Education

Early childhood education seeks to strengthen a child's physical, psychological, and intellectual development. Early childhood education may be offered at childcare facilities to children up to three years of age, and through preschools for children ages four through six. In the new National Guidelines for Education, integration between childcare and preschool has been called "Centers for Early Childhood Education."

Compulsory Education

Education is compulsory between the ages of seven and fourteen. (See table A.3 in the appendix.)

Elementary and secondary curricula include the Portuguese language, mathematics, knowledge of the physical and natural world, as well as political and social studies, providing primarily national information. Physical and artistic education is also compulsory. Environmental education does not constitute a specific discipline on its own and must be integrated across all subject matters. Technological education should also begin at the elementary level. Religious studies are supported by law in Brazil and are offered as electives in public schools.

Elementary Education

Elementary education seeks to develop a student's ability to read, write, and do arithmetic. It is seen as one of the basic tools for human development. Teaching at this level must be carried out in the Portuguese language. In fifth grade, children start learning a foreign language.

Secondary Education

Secondary education spans a period of four years. It aims to deepen and consolidate the knowledge acquired in elementary schooling, preparing the student to continue learning, to think independently and to grasp the basic methodology behind various technological and scientific processes.

Secondary education also includes technical education. Technical education is offered at institutions specifically tailored to deliver technical and/or professional training at the high school level and issue certificates of proficiency in industry, commerce, agriculture, and services. These schools are open to students who have successfully completed their elementary education.

Post-secondary Education

Higher education managed by public institutions (federal, state, and municipal) or private (parochial or secular) accomplishes its goals through teaching, research, cultural events, and extension. Its goals are to promote critical reflection, participation in material production through the specific professions, synthesization, and the advancement of practical and theoretical knowledge.[5] Higher education strives to supply every individual with the basic skills necessary to participate in society as an informed citizen, and also the means to progress in the workplace or in further education.

Brazilian education consists of undergraduate studies, graduate study programs and post-doctoral programs. The University of Brazil enjoys scientific freedom as well as organizational and financial autonomy.

The University of Rio de Janeiro was Brazil's first university, founded in 1920. The University of São Paulo followed in 1934. In 1994 there were 127 universities in Brazil. Each state (except the newest ones) has a federal university. There are state universities in most of the states in the northeast, southeast, and south. The Roman Catholic Church also has some universities, many of them in São Paulo state.

Private Schools

In addition to public education, the government of Brazil acknowledges and authorizes private organizations to support institutions of learning. Thus, parents or guardians have the ability to choose what type of school their child will attend. Private schools in Brazil depend almost exclusively on monthly student tuition and fees. Over the past several years, tuition increases have caused protests, strikes, and even the closing of some schools.

Financing Education

Education is free in official primary and secondary schools. The government must invest at least 18 percent of its tax revenue to the maintenance and development of education annually, and states and municipalities are required to spend at least 25 percent. Public resources generally support public schools, but resources can also be allocated to community, parochial, and philanthropic schools. However, nutritional programs as well as health, transportation, and instructional materials are expected to be financed by other budgetary sources.[6]

Primary education is also supported by funds from the compulsory taxation of businesses, which are specifically earmarked for education. As of 1996, industrial and commercial enterprises contributed 2.5 percent of the sum of all employees' salaries to education. Rural producers and agricultural businesses contributed 0.8 percent of their production.

Adult Education

For young men and women of the working class who do not have access to elementary education at the appropriate age, supplemental education courses have been created, some of which have been offered through distance educational programs. The new Guidelines provide for a special working schedule for the working student population including programs in the workplace, regular course offerings in the evening, a flexible school organization, subject matters centering around the worker's social practice and work, and teaching-learning methods adequate to the student experiences and intellectual development.[7]

Alternative Forms of Education

Distance education is a form of teaching among Brazilians that is not well-developed but which has great potential. It provides students with the opportunity for independent study, giving them the freedom to create their own schedules and to combine self-teaching instructional materials with access to modern means of communication without leaving the home. Distance education, however, requires a great deal of discipline on the student's behalf.

Because of its specific characteristics, distance education when applied to early childhood and elementary schooling is not very effective. It is predominately offered to young men and women and to working-class adults. Distance education has the characteristics of continuing education, professional training, and cultural enrichment.

Literacy Rates

The level of adult literacy is similar for both sexes. In 1950, only half of the population over fifteen years of age was literate. A literacy campaign begun in 1971 raised this to the current level of 85 percent. Literacy levels vary regionally between rural and urban areas. Illiteracy is highest—around 40 percent—in the northeast, which has a high proportion of rural people. The 1991 census revealed that 19 percent of the urban populations over the age of ten were illiterate, as opposed to 46 percent of the rural population.

School Enrollment Rates

In Brazil, the proportion of children attending school decreases with age. While almost all children between the ages of seven and fourteen are in school, the share of secondary school-aged children enrolled falls to 62 percent. (See tables A.4, A.5, A.6, and A.7 in the appendix.) In many instances, children do not attend school because they are forced to work to support their families. (See figure 3.5.)

Reforms in the Current Educational System

Despite the progressive nature of Brazil's legislation on education and the often progressive thinking of Brazilian educators, the country still has one of the lowest-performing educational systems in the world. Drastic changes in teaching and funding are needed to make the education system more viable. These changes, as well as stronger efforts to

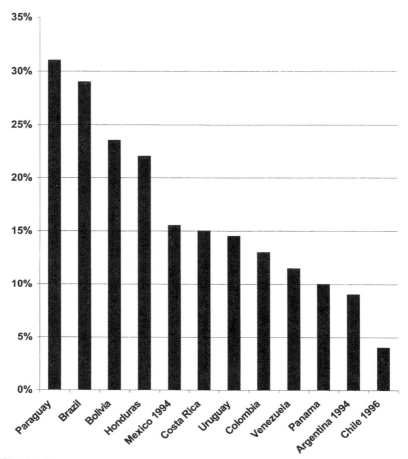

FIGURE 3.5
Percentage of Boys, Girls, and Adolescents Ages 13–17 Who Work, 1997

reduce the illiteracy rates among Brazilian citizens are the major policy goals of the country.

Notes

1. Moacir Gadotti, "Contemporary Brazilian Education: Challenges of Basic Education" in Carlos Alberto Torres and Adriana Puiggros, eds., *Latin American Education* (Boulder, Colo.: Westview Press, 1997).

2. Brazilian Constitution.
3. Ibid.
4. Gadotti, "Contemporary Brazilian Education: Challenges of Basic Education."
5. Ibid.
6. Ibid.
7. Ibid.

ARGENTINA

Background Information

The Federal Republic of Argentina is the second largest country in South America, and occupies much of the southern portion of the continent. It is a major agricultural producer, but is also highly industrialized, with the vast majority of its citizens (86 percent) living in urban centers.

Argentina is a federal republic headed by a president, who is assisted by a Council of Ministers. Legislative powers are vested in a national congress consisting of a Senate and a Chamber of Deputies. All constitutional provisions have been repeatedly suspended and then reinstated. As of 1994, several parts of Argentina's Constitution were revised, although the basic system of government remained unchanged.

Argentina is a nation with a rich Spanish heritage. Spanish is the official language and is spoken by the overwhelming majority of Argentines. Italian and a number of Native American languages are also spoken.

Roman Catholics make up the 90 percent of the population, and the church plays a major role in shaping the country's laws and policies, especially those concerning women's issues.

Basis of the Educational System—Principles and Legislation

The Argentine Constitution mandates seven years of free, compulsory primary school education for all girls and boys until the age of fourteen.

One way in which the status of women can be readily observed is by the manner in which a country educates its female citizens. In 1991, the Argentine government created the National Program for the Promotion of Equal Opportunities for Women in the Educational Area. Its main goals include revising the national curriculum to make it less gender-biased and ensuring equal opportunities for women.

Organization of the Educational System

The educational system of Argentina operates on a three-tiered system beginning with non-compulsory preschool education, followed by compulsory education, consisting of primary and secondary schools. Post-secondary education is the third tier of the educational system in Argentina consisting of universities, as well as vocational and technical schools.

Pre-primary Education

Pre-primary education in Argentina is available for children before the age of five. The aim of preschool is to teach children basic skills and habits that will help them in adapting and integrating into further education.

Compulsory Education

Primary education in Argentina is free and compulsory from ages five to fourteen. (See table A.3 in the appendix.) Children are required to attend school for ten years. But most children do not finish compulsory education due to poverty. Poverty affects millions of children in Latin America and 35 percent of the poor in Latin America are under the age of fifteen. The number of poor persons in Latin America has increased drastically in the last two decades. In 1997, there were 204 million people living in poverty in Latin America, of whom 100 million could not even satisfy their basic nutritional needs. Most children leave school to work in order to help support their families. (See figure 3.5 on page 42 of this book.)

Primary and Secondary Education

In primary and secondary school, children learn the basic skills that they will need to enter the work force or advance to higher education. Most children do not complete formal education in Argentina. This is in part due to the economic difficulties within families that force children to work.

Post-secondary Education

Argentina, like Brazil, has been influenced and conditioned by an international agenda for the modernization of its higher education systems. The Argentine Higher Education Law No. 24.521 was promulgated in August 1995, and targets all institutions of higher education universities or non-universities, national, provincial or municipal, state-owned or private. All form part of the National Educational System regulated by

Law No. 24.195, which introduced substantial changes in the autonomy, financing, and governance of universities. For example, the law authorized university institutions to establish their own system of admissions and graduation.[1]

Argentina has twenty-five national universities and many private universities. The principal institution is the University of Buenos Aires. In 1987, the University established a post-graduate women's study program to improve the status of women throughout Argentina. Other universities, including the National University of Comahue and the University of Cuyo, have similar programs.

Private Schools

Private schools are funded by tuition fees. Argentina is a relatively poor country, and only the wealthy can afford to send their children to private institutions. For those who can afford it, however, private institutions are an available option for children at all levels of education.

Financing Education

Public education is free for all citizens in Argentina. At the university and higher-level education, public funding decreases drastically and individuals pay the majority of the costs, with only a small amount of help from the government.

Literacy Rates

Literacy rates for adults tend to be lower in the rural areas, where only about 10 percent of girls attend secondary school and only 2 percent go on to college. Nevertheless, average literacy rates for the country as a whole are 96 percent for both men and women. (See table 4.1 in the appendix.)

School Enrollment Rates

On average, girls spend slightly more time in school than boys: nine-and-one-half years for girls, compared to nine years for boys. At the primary level, about 95 percent of all girls are enrolled in school, with the number of girls equaling the number of boys. But as these students progress through the educational system, more boys tend to drop out and enter the job market. Twenty percent of boys and girls enter the educational system late, 42 percent repeat first grade, and 30 percent repeat second grade. The average repetition of school years in all primary school grades is 30 percent per year. Statistics show that many children in Argentina do not complete primary school.

In 1997, 5.5 million pupils attended primary school and 2.6 million attended secondary and vocational schools. (See tables A.4, A.5, A.6, and A.7 in the appendix.)

Reforms in the Current Educational System

In Argentina, policy makers, educators, and others involved in the educational system are trying to create more equality and efficiency within the school system. They are trying to eradicate illiteracy and provide a basic quality education for all children.

Note

1. See <http://www.unicef.org/lac/ingles/infancia/edupri.htm>.

Country Profiles: Western Europe

GREAT BRITAIN

Background Information

Great Britain occupies the island located off the mainland of Europe in the Atlantic Ocean. Although it is one of Europe's smallest countries, it is one of the most urban and most densely populated.

Great Britain is a constitutional monarchy and the monarch is the Sovereign Head of State and Head of Government. The government is comprised of the Legislature (Parliament), the Executive, and the Judiciary. Parliament consists of the House of Lords and the House of Commons. Most of the work of Parliament is conducted in the House of Commons at Westminster. The Prime Minister is the active head of the government. The official language of instruction and use is English.

Every major religion is represented in Great Britain. The majority of people are Protestant, followed by Roman Catholics. The rest are made up of Muslims, Hindus, Sikhs, Jews, and many other religions.

Basis of the Educational System—Principles and Legislation

Education legislation provides that all children between the ages of five and sixteen must receive full-time education suitable to their age, ability, and aptitude, and adapted to any special educational need they may have. All children between the ages of five and sixteen are entitled to free compulsory education. Any subsequent full-time education is also free for students up to the age of nineteen. Students attending institutions of higher education may have to make a contribution toward tuition fees.

The Educational Reform Act of 1988 introduced for the first time a national curriculum for schools. This Act also provided for a higher level of financial autonomy in the schools. The Further and Higher Education Act of 1992 abolished the distinction between universities and polytechnics, and established new funding councils for both further and higher education. It also transferred further educational institutions from local authority control to corporate bodies. The bulk of the law of education as it relates to schools is now contained in the Education Act of 1996, which repealed and consolidated earlier legislation without changing its effect. The School Standards and Framework Act of 1998 introduced measures to raise the standards of education, and created a new framework of community, foundation, and voluntary schools.[1]

Control of the Educational System

The Department for Education and Employment (DfEE) carries out the administration of education at a national level. At the municipal level, local education authorities, as well as education and library boards are responsible for organizing publicly-funded education within their area. Further and higher education institutions are fully autonomous. Overall, educational institutions enjoy a high degree of autonomy.

The provision and organization of education and adult education services is the responsibility of the 172 democratically elected local councils in Great Britain and Wales that have designated responsibility as local education authorities (LEAs). Most LEAs have an educational committee, which determines and monitors their responsibilities. Issues of concern include the numbers of schools, budgets, admission policies, transportation, and arrangements for special educational needs.

Organization of the Educational System

Education in Great Britain begins at the pre-primary level. Pre-primary education begins around the age of two-and-one-half years with pre-primary groups and playgroups. Nursery schools accept children from around the age of three. Many children attend, although it is not mandatory. The educational system is predominantly a two-tier system of primary and secondary education. In some areas, a three-tier system is operational; children are promoted from primary school to middle school at the age of eight or nine and to a secondary school at the age of twelve or thirteen. Some primary schools (known as infant schools) cater to children up to seven years of age. Others, known as junior schools, cater to children ages seven through eleven. The vast majority of secondary schools are comprehensive schools and do not select students on their abilities. Grammar schools, however, select children on ability. Higher education and other forms of post-secondary education vary widely and consist of colleges, tertiary colleges, specialist colleges, and adult education centers.

Pre-primary Education

Pre-primary, nursery, or early education in Great Britain is currently undergoing reforms. This is a result of government commitment to expand publicly-funded pre-primary education and to integrate nursery school education with preprimary childcare and out-of-school care.

Nursery education is full- or part-time education for children five years of age and younger. It aims to emphasize early literacy, numbers, and the development of personal and social skills, and generally contribute to children's knowledge, understanding, and skills in other areas before they begin compulsory schooling. Although student participation in nursery education is not compulsory, it is widespread and increasing.

Four types of educational opportunities exist for children between three months and five years of age: day nurseries (up to four or five years of age), preschool groups or play groups (from two-and-one-half to four or five years of age), nursery schools or classes (from three to four or five years of age), and reception classes at primary school (from age four). The government is currently expanding and developing publicly funded early-year education through cooperation with the private sector. Nursery school is provided free of charge to most four-year-olds in private establishments. School for three-year-olds is funded at the discretion of the LEA.[2]

Compulsory Education

Great Britain mandates compulsory full-time education for children aged five to sixteen. Children can either be educated at school or at home. (See table A.3 in the appendix.)

Compulsory education is divided into four stages: stage 1 (ages five to seven), stage 2 (ages seven to eleven), stage 3 (ages eleven to fourteen) and stage 4 (ages fourteen to sixteen).

Within the predominant two-tier system of primary and secondary education, stages 1 and 2 are provided in primary school, and stages 3 and 4 are provided in secondary school. Although many secondary schools only cater to pupils up to the end of compulsory education (age sixteen), over half also provide post-compulsory education up to and even over the age of eighteen.[3]

Primary School

Primary schools have the authority to develop their own curriculum to reflect the particular needs and circumstances of their students. But every publicly-funded primary school must provide the National Curriculum, religious education, and collective worship to all pupils. At the request of the parent, a student may be withdrawn from collective worship and religious education. In primary school, children learn basic concepts in mathematics, English, science, history, geography, art, music, and physical education. The amount of time spent on each subject is not mandated. At the end of stage 1 (age seven) students undertake practical classroom-based tasks and written tests in English and mathematics. At the end of stage 2 (age eleven) pupils take a written test in English, mathematics, and science.

Secondary School

In secondary school, students are required to follow a National Curriculum that includes the continuation of subjects from primary school with the addition of foreign languages and sexual education. Parents may waive their child's participation in sex education. At the secondary-school level, teachers consistently monitor the child's progress. At the end of each stage, a cumulative examination is administered.

Post-secondary Education

Post-compulsory education for sixteen- to nineteen-year-olds is provided in secondary schools, where it is considered to be secondary education, and also in further educational institutions. The Further and Higher Education Act of 1992 defines "further education" as "full-time and part-time education suitable to the requirements of persons over compulsory school age including vocational, social, physical and recreational training." Post-compulsory education is provided free of charge to students up to the age of nineteen.

For post-secondary education, schools and sixth form colleges offer more general education; further educational colleges offer largely vocational education; and tertiary colleges offer a combination of general and vocational education. Many secondary schools provide education for pupils from ages eleven to sixteen or eighteen and cover both lower and upper secondary education.

There are no formal qualifications for admission to post-compulsory education, although schools and colleges may set specific requirements relating to General Certificate of Secondary Education (GCSE) results for admission to individual courses. Students may apply to any institution offering their choice of study. There are no compulsory subjects at this level. Students choose courses of study from those offered by the school or further educational institution based on the qualification they seek.

Higher Education

Students who wish to go on to university or other higher educational institutions usually study subjects which lead to taking the General Certificate of Education-Advanced (GCE-A level), which is the main external examination offered in schools at the post-compulsory education level. The GCE-A examination is also available and is equivalent to one half of a GCE-A level.

All higher educational institutions are legally independent, autonomous entities that determine their own admission policies and requirements. In most cases, applicants require 2 GCE-A level, General National Vocation Qualifications (GNVQ), or equivalent qualifications. The governing body of a higher education institution has full responsibility for curriculum and internal organization. All universities and certain other higher-education institutions have the ability to award their own degrees.

University students generally work towards a first Bachelors degree during their three- or four-year course, but many institutions also offer subdegree level courses such as BTEC Higher National Diplomas.

Private Schools

Parents are free to choose which type of educational institution their child will attend. Schools outside the public sector are known as independent schools. Some long-established senior (secondary) schools are known as public schools. Most boarding schools are independent schools. Approximately 7 percent of the students in Great Britain attend independent schools.

Independent schools receive no direct state funding, but are financed from fees and income from investments. Boards of Governors at not-for-profit organizations run the majority of independent schools. Independent schools must be registered with the Department for Education and Employment (DfEE), which can require them to remedy deficiencies in their premises, accommodations, or instruction. Independent schools are not required to implement the National Curriculum, but they must satisfy inspectors that their curriculum is on par with those in the public sector.

Financing Education

All publicly-funded compulsory education in Great Britain is free of charge. Public sector schools receive their funding from LEAs. All publicly-funded schools are fully funded for capital expenditure.

Local authorities are free to decide how much of the total revenue available to devote to education. The majority of these resources are received from the central government, based on the government's standard assessment of the authorities expenditure needs as compared with the income it raises locally. The rest comes from the local authority self-financed sources, primarily the Council tax.[4]

All institutions of higher education charge fees. Many students are eligible for financial assistance, including loans. Awards for post-graduate work may be obtained for approved courses in advanced studies and for research.

Adult Education

Adult education services that provide part-time courses fall under the responsibility of LEAs. Thus, the way in which adult education services are organized can vary greatly. For example, there may be freestanding adult education centers; integrated community education services offered through schools; or further education institutions under contract to the LEA.

Literacy Rates

Literacy rates in Great Britain, at 99 percent, are among the highest in the world. This is due to Britain's strong commitment to education. Compulsory education lasts for eleven years. Currently there is legislation pending to make pre-primary education compulsory as well.

School Enrollment Rates

School enrollment in Great Britain is high. Approximately 5.3 million children attend primary schools; 6.5 million attend secondary school, and 1.8 million attend tertiary school. (See tables A.4, A.5, A.6, and A.7 in the appendix.) The rates of participation in higher education are also relatively high. (See table 3.7.)

TABLE 3.7
Rates of Participation in Higher Education

Higher-education students, 1996–1997	England	Wales
Undergraduate students, 1996–1997		
Full-time	807,138	57,192
Part-time	352,459	20,018
Total	1,159,597	77,210
Post-graduate students, 1996–1997		
Full-time	115,729	7,030
Part-time	183,358	10,449
Total	299,087	17,479
Academic staff 1996–1997		
Full-time	89,551	5,363
Part-time	14,405	637
Total	103,956	6,000

Continued

TABLE 3.7 *Continued*

Higher-education students, 1996–1997	England	Wales
Higher-education institutions, 1998		
Universities*	89	9
Higher-education colleges**	44	4
Total	133	13

* England figure includes the privately funded University of Buckingham and the constituent colleges of the University of London. Wales figure includes the constituent colleges and universities of the University of Wales
** Includes teacher training colleges

Reforms in the Current Educational System

Recent educational reforms in Great Britain include the setting up of the National Learning and Skills Council to assume responsibility for all education and training after the age of sixteen (excluding higher education). The National Council will work through a network of up to fifty local Learning and Skills Councils, create a new simplified system of funding education and training for those over sixteen years of age, and change inspection arrangements of daycare, preschools, post-sixteen schools and colleges. The Council will also seek to raise standards, encourage diversity, and increase access to and participation in education.

Notes

1. *Structures of Education, Initial Training and Adult Education Systems in Europe.* (United Kingdom: Eurydice Unit in Great Britain and Scotland and member of the CEDEFOP Documentary Network Institute of Personnel and Development, 1999).
2. Ibid.
3. Ibid.
4. Ibid.

ITALY

Background Information

Italy, in southern Europe, is a long peninsula extending into the Mediterranean Sea. The country includes two large islands, Sardinia and Sicily, and several smaller ones. Italy covers an area of 301,341 square kilometers. In January 1997, Italy's population was 57,563,354. It is homogenous and approximately two-thirds of Italians live in cities.

Italy is a parliamentary republic controlled by a president and a parliament. The Parliament, which exercises legislative power, consists of the Chamber of Deputies and a Senate.

For administrative purposes, Italy is divided into twenty autonomous territories, known as regions. Each of these regions possesses its own legislative, administrative, and financial powers. The regions are further divided into provinces, each of which consists of a number of communes linked to an urban center. At both the provincial and communal levels, administration is in the hands of elected officials.

Italian is the official language of Italy, although in some areas the use of the local language on official documents and in education is authorized.

Vatican City is located in Rome, the center of Roman Catholicism. Eighty-four percent of Italians claim at least a nominal affiliation to Catholicism. Although Roman Catholicism is no longer the formal state religion, the church remains a strong political force. Yet over the years, its influence on Italian laws and policies has diminished, especially in such matters as divorce, birth control, and abortion.

Basis of the Educational System—Principles and Legislation

The basic principles relating to education are provided for in the Italian Constitution, including: freedom of education; the State's duty to provide a network of educational establishments of every type and level open to all without distinction; the right of private individuals to set up schools at no cost to the State; the right and duty of parents to educate their children for at least eight years; and the right to education and vocational assistance for those who are incapacitated or handicapped. In addition, the Constitution provides that, "those possessing capacity and merit, even if they lack the means, have the right to attain the highest level of study" (Art. 34 of the Italian Constitution).[1]

Control of the Educational System

Responsibility for pre-primary, primary, and secondary education in Italy belongs to the Ministry of Education and the Ministry of University and Scientific and Technological Research. The Ministry is represented at local levels by regional and provincial education offices. Regions may delegate certain responsibilities to the provinces and municipalities. As of the 2000–2001 school year, all schools have autonomy in the field of administration, organization, pedagogy, research, experimentation, and development.

In higher education, private sectors comprise university institutions, promoted and managed by bodies and private citizens, authorized by the Ministry of University Scientific and Technological Research to issue academic qualifications equivalent to state qualifications. State financial support for private institutions amounts to approximately 20 percent of the total income.

Universities have gained a certain amount of autonomy from the Ministry in administrative, financial and accounting matters. Since 1994, public and private universities have managed their own budgets, and the tasks of the Ministry include the allocation of funds, monitoring and evaluation.[2]

Organization of the Educational System

The educational system of Italy begins as early as three months of age in *Aglio Nido*, or day care facilities. At the age of three, children may enter nursery school where they learn basic skills. At the age of six, children enter *scuola elementare* for five years. They then take an exam, *l'esame della quinta*. It is both written and oral in math and science. If they successfully complete the exam, students advance to middle school, *scuola media*, for three years, and then they take another oral and written exam. *Scuola Superiore* follows, which is field-directed and lasts for five years. There are five disciplines a student can choose to study: *liceo classico*, Latin, Greek, law or humanities studies; *liceo scientifico*, Latin, math, and sciences, which attracts students pursuing a law or medical degree; *liceo linguistico*, study of languages; *liceo technico*, involving vocational studies, and *magistrali* (which is a four-year program) for elementary education. After the third and fifth years an exam is administered, *l'esame di maturità*, which is both written and oral. Students are then free to enter universities, which are course specific. Receiving a diploma from a university in Italy is equivalent to receiving a master's degree in the United States. If a student desires further specialization, they most often go abroad.[3]

Pre-primary Education (*Aglio Nido* and *Scuola Materna*)

Parents who work may send their children to day care centers starting at the age of three months. These include state-run institutions that are free of charge, as well as private institutions requiring some form of payment. Pre-primary education is not compulsory, but many Italians recognize it as a crucial stage in the education process. On average, 97.8 percent of children aged three to six years attend nursery schools, with a small percentage of enrollments in state schools. Children gain strength in physical, intellectual, and psychodynamic characteristics which help them to develop sensorial, perceptive, motor, linguistics and intellectual abilities.

Compulsory Education

Article 34 of the Italian Constitution provides that, "lower education dispensed for at least eight years is compulsory and free of charge."[4] As of January 20, 1999, the duration of compulsory education was increased to nine years. Thus, compulsory education begins at the age of six and continues until age fifteen: five years of primary education, three years of lower secondary, and one year of upper secondary education. There has been a long-standing proposal in Italy to extend the age of compulsory education to age eighteen. (See table A.3 in the appendix.)

Scuola Elementare and *Scuola Media*

Six-year-old children are eligible to attend primary school (*scuola elementare*). Normally children attend the school nearest to their home. In primary school, students are taught the principles outlined in the Italian Constitution, cultural traditions, reading and writing, mathematics, science, geography, history, art education, music, and physical education. Catholic religion classes are optional. Students must have a primary school certificate to be admitted to *scuola media*. It is at this level that foreign language is introduced. The aim of *scuola media* is to broaden their educational base.

Upper Secondary School and Post-compulsory Education

At the upper secondary and post-compulsory level of education, the course of study which students decide to pursue is field directed. Students may choose between five courses of study. *Liceo classico*, Latin, Greek (attracting students who will go into law or humanities studies); *liceo scientifico*, Latin, math, sciences (attracting pupils who will go into law or medicine); *liceo linguistico* (study of languages); *liceo technico* (vocational studies); and *magistrali* (a four-year program for elementary education). After the third and fifth years an exam is administered, *l'esame di maturità*, which is both written and oral.

Higher Education

There are two main types of higher education: university education, which offers a wide range of degrees and courses, and non-university, which has its own structure, regulations, and organization. Students must have an upper secondary education to be admitted to either. The age of admission varies from institution to institution. University courses lead to four types of academic titles: a diploma *universitario* (two or three years), a *laurea* (courses ranging from four to six years), a diploma of specialization (from two to four years), and a research doctorate (three years). Access to specialization or a research doctorate requires the *laurea* and is regulated by exams.

Private Schools

Article 33 of the Italian Constitution allows for the establishment of private schools. The state gives broad guidelines for the establishment of non–state-run schools, but private schools must comply with state regulations on health and curriculum.

There are two categories of non-state schools. These are non–state-authorized schools that are managed by corporations or associations with legal status. Authorized private schools are managed by citizens possessing upper secondary school qualifications and who are shown to be legally and morally capable. Both types of schools need approval and authorization from the educational director.

Financing Education

Funds for public education come directly from the Ministry of Public Education. Technical and vocational schools use funds directly allocated by the Ministry of Public Education for necessary expenditure and purchases needed for operating agricultural schools, laboratories and facilities attached to those schools.

Adult Education

There are two main organizations that provide adult education classes. The first of them falls under the responsibility of the Ministry of Public Education. The second provides continuing vocational training for adult workers and is organized by regional authorities. Both are designed to keep and further the educational level of adults.

Literacy Rates

Literacy rates in Italy are among the highest in the world. Both men and women are 99 percent literate. In recent years, however, there have been a large number of immigrants and gypsies who have contributed to an increase in the illiteracy rates. (See table A.1 in the appendix.)

School Enrollment Rates

The school enrollment rate drastically decreases at the tertiary level. At the secondary level, enrollments are 4,602,243, and at the primary level enrollments are only 2,816,128. (See table 3.8 and tables A.4, A.5, A.6, and A.7 in the appendix.)

TABLE 3.8
Number of Students in the 1997–1998 School Year

1997–1998 school year	
State schools:	
Number of pupils per teacher	11.7
Number of pupils per section	23.4
Pupils	917,881
Teachers	81,273
Schools	13,624
Sections	39,283

Source: Ministero della Pubblica Istruzione, La scuola statale: sintesi del dati, 1998; ISTAT, Annuario Statistico Italiano, 1998

Reforms of the Current Educational System

The Italian Ministry of Education seeks to implement school autonomy, reorganize school cycles and reform the curricula. The Ministry also wants to extend the compulsory age of education to eighteen years of age, and mandate seven years of basic school education and five years of secondary school.

Notes

1. Italian Constitution.
2. Ibid.
3. Professor Ponce de Leon. Lecture on "Education in Italy." American University of Rome, spring 2000.
4. Italian Constitution.

GERMANY

Background Information

The Federal Republic of Germany sits in the center of Western Europe surrounded by Austria, Italy, and France. It is the most populous country in Western Europe, with a population of 81.2 million people, and is one of the world's leading economic powers. Germany covers 357,000 square kilometers. The size of Germany's territory increased on October 3, 1990, as a result of German unification based on a treaty between the Federal Republic of Germany (West Germany) and the communist-ruled German Democratic Republic (East Germany).

Germany is made up of sixteen *Lander*, or states. The former East Germany compromised five states, now called the new *Lander*. The eleven states from West Germany, now referred to as the old *Lander*, house about 80 percent of the total population. In both the old and new *Lander*, the great majority of people live in urban centers (76 percent). The predominant responsibility for education belongs to the *Lander*. Each *Lander* has its own constitution and government.

Under the *Grudgesetz* (Basic Law), the *Bundestag* (Federal German Parliament) and the *Brudesrat* (composed of members of government in the *Lander*) are the constitutional bodies with legislative authority. The federal government generally carries out executive functions in the field of homeland and foreign affairs. The federal government is headed by the federal chancellor and is composed of fifteen ministers. The federal president is the Head of State and is elected for a five-year term.[1]

The official language of Germany is German and education is conducted primarily in German.

German law guarantees freedom of creed, conscience, religion, and ideological persuasion. There is no established state church. Protestants make up about 49 percent of the population, and tend to live in northern regions of Germany. About 45 percent of Germans are Roman Catholics.

Basis of the Educational System—Principles and Legislation

According to the Basic Law, Germany is a republic and a democracy. In education, the Basic law guarantees, among other things, the freedom of art and science, research and training, the freedom of creed and conscience, the freedom to profess a religion, the freedom to choose one's occupation, and place of study and training, equality before the law, and the natural rights of parents to care for and to raise up their children.

The *Lander* is responsible for exercising State powers and fulfilling State obligations. The *Lander* is thus entitled to pass legislation where the Basic Law does not grant legislative power to the Federation (*Bund*). The Constitution and the laws of the *Lander* govern pre-primary institutions, the school system and higher education, adult education, and continuing education.

Control of the Educational System

According to the Basic Law, educational legislation and administration are primarily the responsibility of the *Lander*. This is particularly so with regard to the school system, higher education, and the adult education/continuing education sector. Among these responsibilities are legislation concerning general rules for tertiary education, the promotion of individual training, including the promotion of younger academic staff. The Basic Law also provides for particular forms of cooperation between the Federation and the *Lander*, such as with educational planning and the promotion of research.

Two-thirds of all students train in the *Dualen* System, a dual system of vocational training in both the workplace and at school. The workplace activity is financed by firms, and the school element by the *Lander*. The workplace activity follows nationally coordinated rules for training, while there are curricula for the school-based work, which are established by the *Lander*.

Public institutions, such as Chambers of Industry and Commerce, and Chambers of Craftsmanship, supervise vocational training in the workplace.[2]

Organization of the Educational System

The educational system begins at the pre-primary level with kindergarten for children between the ages of three and six. While it is not compulsory, many children attend kindergarten. At the age of six children enter primary school. Primary education (*Grundschuen*) is from first to the fourth school year (in Berlin and Brandenburg until the sixth year).

General Secondary lower schools build on primary education. In most *Lander* these are the *Hauptschule, Realschule, Gymnasium,* and *Gesamtschule.* The education available for sixteen- to nineteen-year-olds at the upper secondary level include: General Upper Secondary Education; *Gymnasiale Oberstufe,* which covers years eleven through thirteen and is usually subdivided into a one-year introductory phase and a two-year qualification phase; vocational education and training, which is full time and mixes general and vocational education.[3]

Tertiary-level education includes various types of university and, to a limited degree, non-university institutions. Some *Lander* offer professional academies alongside higher-education institutions. They offer upper secondary school graduates higher-education training courses leading to a profession as an alternative to university studies.

Pre-primary Education

In most *Lander,* responsibility for preschool education lies with the social ministries. From three to six years of age, children can attend kindergartens, which are mainly run by non-public bodies (churches and welfare associations). There are also other types of institutions but attendance is low. They tend to be for those children who are not ready or fully developed by the time they reach compulsory school age. Parents are expected to contribute money, despite the allocation of major public subsidies and reliance on other funds. Pre-primary education is not a part of the statutory school system.

Compulsory Education

- *Grundschule* (primary education)   Six to ten years of age
                                           Six to twelve in Berlin and
                                              Brandenburg

Lower Secondary Education

- *Orientierungsstufe* (Orientation   Ten to twelve years of age
  phase within the different
  school types or as a separate
  organizational unit)

• *Gymnasium/Realschule/Hauptschule/ Gesamtschule* types of schools offering several courses of education	Twelve to fifteen or sixteen years of age

Upper Secondary Education

• General Upper secondary school, *Gymnasiale Oberstufe*	Sixteen to nineteen years of age
• Vocational Education (full-time)	Fifteen or sixteen to eighteen years of age
• *Dualen* System Dual System: part time vocational school and part time on the job training	Fifteen or sixteen to eighteen or nineteen years of age

Full-time education in Germany is compulsory starting at the age of six and extending, depending on the Lander, for nine years, or ten years in Berlin, Brandenburg, and Nordrhein-Westfalen. Part-time education is compulsory until the age of eighteen. For those who do not wish to continue education, the *Lander* establishes vocational training schools that are compulsory.

Primary Education

Primary education is provided at Grundschuen from first to the fourth school year (in Berlin and Brandenburg until the sixth year). At this level, the goal is to establish a more systematic form of learning, and teach broad subject matters. Primary education lays the foundation for further schooling. The transition from primary school to secondary school is subject to different regulations depending on legislation in the individual *Lander*. The parents, on the basis of an assessment made by the primary school, decide on the type of school their children will attend at the lower secondary level. Admission to the various types of secondary schools may be subject to students fulfilling certain performance criteria and/or a decision by the education authority.

General Secondary Lower Education

General Secondary lower schools build on primary education. In most *Lander* these are the *Hauptschule, Realschule, Gymnasium,* and *Gesamtschule.* In recent years some *Lander* have introduced new types of schooling with different names depending on the Lander. These new schools combine the educational paths of the *Houtschule* and the *Realschule* into one organizational and educational unit. The principle underlying different types of lower secondary education is to give students a basic general education, combined with an element of individual specialization. At various times throughout lower secondary education, observation and orientation towards further specialization occurs.

Schools offering one educational path include *Hauptschule*, the *Realschule*, and the *Gymnasium*. The *Hauptschule* provides pupils with a fundamental general education. It covers the fifth through ninth year. Students may stay for another year to receive a certificate to acquire further qualification. The *Realschule* offers pupils an extended general education. It normally covers the fifth through tenth year. The *Realschule* certificate allows for transition into training courses resulting directly in vocational qualifications or school types providing a higher entrance qualification. *Gymnasium* offers pupils an intensified general education. It normally covers the fifth through thirteenth year. Students usually attain the general higher education entrance qualification after completion of the gymnasium.

There are also school types that offer more than one educational path and they often differ among *Lander*s. The *Gesamtschule*, for example, combines all three of the previously mentioned schools into one educational unit giving the student more opportunities for the future.[4]

Upper Secondary Education

Education available for sixteen to nineteen-year-olds at the upper secondary level include: general upper secondary education, vocational education and training, which is full-time; and mixed general and vocational education.

Admission to the *Gymnasiale Oberstufe* (upper level *Gymnasium*) requires a lower secondary level qualification and attainment of certain standards of achievement. Students in the *Gymnasiale Oberstufe* must study subjects from three groups: languages/literature/the arts; social sciences; and mathematics/natural sciences/technology. The general upper secondary education, *Gymnasiale Oberstufe* covers years eleven through thirteen and is usually subdivided into a one-year introductory phase and a two-year qualification phase. They must have a concentration in two subject areas, one of which must be German, and a continuation of a foreign language, mathematics, or a natural science. Admission requirements for full-time vocational education depend on the type of school chosen. Vocational programs in *Berufsfchschulen* include German, social studies, mathematics, natural sciences, a foreign language and sport, as well as vocational subjects. Full-time vocational schools prepare students for employment while furthering their education. Most attend *Berufsfachschule*, which offer a wide range of courses. There are *Berufsfachschule* for business occupations, occupations specializing in foreign languages, crafts, home economics, social work, art, and health care, among others. The duration of study depends on the career specialization.

The Dual System of Education is open to all lower secondary school levels. It includes part-time vocational school and part-time on-the-job training. The aim is to provide a basic vocational education and the necessary skills and knowledge required for practicing a particular trade or profession. Those successfully completing the training are entitled to practice their occupation as qualified employees in one of the state-recognized occupations for which formal training is required.

At all levels there are examinations that must be passed in order to gain a graduation certificate. These certificates grant access to higher education.[5]

Post-secondary Education

The tertiary level of education includes various types of university and non-university institutions. Some *Lander* offer professional academies alongside higher education institutions. They offer upper secondary school graduates, who are entitled to attend higher education training, courses leading to a profession as an alternative to university studies.

Non-university Institutions

Non-university institutions combine theoretical training in an academic institution with practical vocational training in a business as part of the dual system framework. Students simultaneously maintain relationships with businesses, comparable institutions outside of business (particularly in independent professions), as well as with institutions established by social service providers. The business assumes the cost of vocational training and pays the student a wage. The course of study usually is divided into two years of basic study and one year of advanced study. After passing an examination, the students receive a certificate that allows them employment in the business.[6]

University Education

Germany has several institutions of higher education. A total of 337 existed in the 1997–1998 academic year, which included seventy-five non-state higher-education institutions.

Universities and equivalent higher education institutions offer post doctorate teaching qualifications. They usually range across subjects such as theology, humanities and law, economic and social sciences, natural science and engineering, and agriculture and medicine. Depending on the course of study, one may earn a certificate or have to take an examination.

There are also colleges of education that train teachers as well as colleges of art and music which offer courses in visual design and the performing arts. There are also Universities of Applied Sciences, with the bulk of their courses in the engineering sciences, economics and business, social sciences, information sciences, and communications areas.

In order to gain admission to an institute of higher learning, a certificate from a lower secondary school or vocational institution is necessary. If the number of applications for one course of study is higher than the number of places available, the amount of time one has been on the list is taken into account. Qualifications for entry vary according to the course of study.

Private Schools

The German Constitution grants the right to private education (Art. 7, paragraph 4). It states that private schools will be approved if the teaching goals, equipment, and training are not inferior to that of the public sector and do not promote separation of pupils based on the economic status of their parents. There are two categories of private schools: alternative schools, which substitute for public schools that already exist; and complementary schools, which supplement public education by providing training courses primarily in the vocational sector.

Financing Education

Private schools require payment of tuition. Citizens, the private sector, the public sector, businesses, social groups, continuing education institutions, and public broadcasting companies share the responsibility for helping continuing educational participants. In 1997, all students were in publicly funded schools, 5.1 percent of which are private grant-aided institutions (provided and controlled by non-government bodies).

Adult Education

The state limits itself in the area of continuing education as to the establishing of principles and regulations concerning the support of such organizations. Adult education is an independent area of continuing education providing general education and vocational training.

Literacy Rates

Literacy rates in Germany are among the highest in the world at 99 percent for both men and women, due in part to the fact that students attend twelve years of compulsory education and are tested regularly on their basic skills. (See table A.1 in the appendix.)

School Enrollment Rates

Women make up 42 percent of the students in vocational training systems. The most popular vocations are store clerk, medical and dental assistant, clerical worker, and hairdresser. Only 31 percent of the polytechnic programs include women.

While pre-compulsory education is not mandatory, many attend: age three, 45.7 percent; age four, 78.1 percent; and age five, 87.8 percent. In

TABLE 3.9
Statistics on Higher Education

Institutions of Higher Education by Type of Institution and Land
(Winter semester 1997–1998)

Universities and equivalent institutions of higher education	113
Art and music colleges	46
Fachhochschulen including Fachhochschulen for administrative studies	178
Total	337

Source: *Grund- und Strukturdaten*, 1998–1999

Students by Type of Higher Education Institution
(Winter semester, 1997–1998)*

Universities and equivalent institutions of higher education	1,364,400
Art and music colleges	29,900
Fachhochschulen including Fachhochschulen for administrative studies	438,400
Total	1,832,700
	(29%)

*as a percentage of the 19-to under 26-year-old age group
Source: *Grund- und Strukturdaten*, 1998–1999

Full-time Academic and Artistic Staff* at Institutions of Higher Education, 1996

	Total	Of whom professors
Universities and art and music colleges	137,718	24,569
Fachhochschulen including Fachhochschulen for administrative studies	16,730	13,020
Total	154,448	37,589

*Professors, academic and artistic employees and teaching staff for special tasks
Source: *Grund- und Strukturdaten*, 1998–1999

1993, 54 percent of school-aged children attended primary and secondary school. In higher education, 43 percent were enrolled. (See table 3.9 and tables A.4, A.5, A.6, and A.7 in the appendix.)

Reforms in the Current Educational System

Some reforms that are being discussed in Germany include improving the quality of schools, revamping the curriculum to make it more challenging, enhancing international attractiveness to study in Germany, improving individual financial assistance, strengthening autonomy in higher education, and creating equal educational opportunities for all German citizens.

Notes

1. *Structures of Education, Initial Training and Adult Education Systems in Europe, Germany, 1999. (*Brussels: Eurydice European Union).
2. Ibid.
3. Ibid.
4. Ibid.
5. Ibid.
6. Ibid.

SPAIN

Background Information

Spain is located in southwestern Europe, encompassing a total area of 505,990 kilometers. It is bounded on the northeast by France; on the east, by the Mediterranean Sea; on the west by Portugal and the Atlantic Ocean; and on the north by the Bay of Biscay. In 1998, Spain's population was 39,371,147.

Since the adoption of its 1978 Constitution, Spain has been under democratic rule, with a parliamentary monarchy as its form of government. In 1977, the first democratic elections were held. Since then, various political parties have held power. Legislative power is vested in the *Cortes Generales* (Spanish Parliament) composed of two Houses: Congress and Senate.

Spain consists of seventeen Autonomous Communities or Local Domains. According to the Spanish Constitution, Castilian is the official language of Spain. Together with Castilian, there are other official languages in the corresponding Autonomous Communities. These co-languages are Catalan, Gallego, Valenciano, and Euskera. In those Communities where there is a second official language, both it and Castilian are considered compulsory languages for teaching in all levels of education, except universities. The use of the Autonomous Community language as a teaching language varies in the different Communities, depending on how widespread that language is and on the linguistic policies each Community implements.

There is no official religion in Spain, although a large majority of Spanish citizens are Catholic. Public authorities generally work together with the Catholic Church and other religious institutions.

Basis of the Educational System—Principles and Legislation

The 1978 Constitution established the basic legislative principles for education. It recognized education as a fundamental right that the State must guarantee.

The current reform of the Spanish educational system began in 1983 with the Organic Act on University Reform. After 1983, many reforms were enacted, including the 1990 Organic Act on General Organization of the Educational System (LOGSE). Its broad aims are the effective regulation of pre-primary education, thorough reform of vocational training, establishing a post-secondary level, and the interconnection of specialized education in arts and language and other kinds of education.

Control of the Educational System

The State administration has adopted a decentralized model established under the 1978 Constitution. This decentralized model divides educational powers into those reserved to the State, those entrusted to the Autonomous Communities, and those commissioned to municipal governments.

The central government maintains responsibility for the general regulation of the system, but since 1978, certain responsibilities have been delegated to the seventeen regional governments (Autonomous Communities), most of which currently exercise full powers over education. Responsibility for the rest remains with the Ministry of Education and Culture (MEC). Each school has a council, comprised of representatives of the teachers and other staff, parents and students, whose responsibilities include the election of the head teacher.[1]

Organization of the Educational System

The first level of education is pre-primary education, which is not compulsory. Pre-primary education is divided into two cycles each lasting three years. At the age of six, children enter into primary education, which is divided into three cycles each lasting two years. Following is secondary education, which consists of two cycles, only one of which must be completed. The *Bachillerato* level comprises general education at the upper secondary level. Intermediate and Vocational training provide specific vocational training for employment. Higher education in Spain consists of universities, non-universities, and higher specific vocational training.

Pre-primary Education

According to the LOGSE, pre-primary education in Spain is referred to as Education Infantile. Education Infantile is the first level of the educational system, but it is not compulsory. The principal objective of this stage is the child's physical, intellectual, emotional, social, and moral development.

It is divided into two cycles: from zero to three years of age and from three to six years of age. Pre-primary centers can be public or private. The only admission requirement is the age of the child. There are no tuition fees in the second stage in the public establishments, but parents are expected to contribute to the costs of textbooks, and catering or transport, depending on their income.

Compulsory Education

According to the LOGSE, compulsory education lasts ten years, between the ages of six and sixteen. It is divided into two educational levels made up of five stages, each lasting two years—the first three for primary education and the next two for lower secondary education. (See table A.3 in the appendix.)

Primary Education

Primary education is organized into three two-year cycles corresponding to ages six to eight, eight to ten, and ten to twelve, respectively. The purpose of primary education is to provide all children with a basic education, giving them the opportunity to acquire a fundamental cultural background, to gain a command of oral expression, as well as of reading, writing and arithmetic, and to assume gradual autonomy in their respective environments.

Establishments may be public or private. Public schools, *colegios de education primaria*, depend on the local community for their upkeep and maintenance. All establishments have to comply with the requirements set forth by the MEC. For each grade there must be at least one class unit with a maximum of twenty-five students, and that grade must provide education in all three cycles. Private establishments are subject to the principle of administrative authorization, and usually also offer pre-primary education and/or secondary and post-compulsory secondary education. They can be granted such authorization if these minimum requirements are met.

All students must be admitted at this level. The only restriction is age. Certain admission criteria, such as family income, attachment area, and siblings at school, apply when there is overcrowding. Students transfer automatically from primary to lower secondary level.

Compulsory Secondary Education

Secundaria Obligatoria (ESO) consists of four school years divided into two two-year cycles, corresponding to ages twelve to fourteen and fourteen to sixteen. The purpose of this stage is to provide all students with basic cultural skills, train them to assume their responsibilities and exercise their rights, and to prepare them either for work or for post-secondary education.

The minimum core curriculum is determined at the state level. The Autonomous Communities establish their own curriculum based on the state minimum core curriculum and schools develop and adapt the curriculum to their own needs. The lower secondary core curriculum covers Spanish language and literature, the official language of the Autonomous Community, a foreign language, mathematics, physical education, natural sciences, plastic and visual education, social studies, geography and history, technology and music. The subject of religion is voluntary for the students.

There is no national or regional system of testing. The minimum core curriculum includes basic guidelines for assessment, which is an integral part of the curriculum. Promotion to the next level of education is the responsibility of the teachers. Students may repeat a year if the teacher deems it necessary. In the first stage or in each of the two academic years of the second stage of lower secondary education, students may stay one more year if they do not attain the objectives. In principle, they may only repeat one year throughout the entire stage.

Upon completion of compulsory education, students receive the certificate of secondary education (*Graduado en Educacion Secundaria*), which grants access to general upper secondary education (*Bachillerato*) or intermediate level specific vocational training (*Formacion Professional Especifica de grado medio*).[2]

Upper Secondary and Post-secondary Education

As of 1990, post-compulsory secondary education is divided into the academic or general branch, and the vocational branch. In addition, specialized education can be studied simultaneously with this post-compulsory secondary education.

General Upper Secondary Education and Vocational Specific Training

The general branch comprises the new *Bachillerato*, which is organized into a two-year course for students ages sixteen to eighteen. In order to qualify, students must have a *Guaduado en Education Secondaria* certificate. This branch has triple purposes: to prepare pupils for University education, for advanced specific Vocational Training, and finally, for introduction in the labor market. These establishments may be publicly or privately funded. There are no tuition fees in publicly funded establishments but parents may be required to pay for materials, transport, or meals, depending on their level of income.[3]

The *Bachillerato* minimum core curriculum is determined at the national level, but the Autonomous Communities educational authorities and the schools develop and adapt the curricula according to their own needs. There are four kinds of *Bachillerato*: arts, natural sciences and health, humanity and social studies, and technology. Spanish language and literature, the official language of the Autonomous Community, history, philosophy, a foreign language, and physical education, are compulsory subjects for all students.

Autonomous Communities education authorities determine the basic national guidelines for vocational training and the curriculum. It most often includes theoretical and practical training organized on a modular basis.

Bachillerato students are assessed throughout the course. Those who fail more than two subjects in the first year or more than three in the second year must repeat the year. Successful students receive the Bachelor diploma. Continuous assessment also applies to the vocational course and successful students receive the *Tecnico* certificate.

Higher Education

Higher education refers to all post-secondary education. It covers university education, advanced-level specific vocational training, and other specialized institutions. University-level education is offered in university faculties, higher technical educational centers, and university centers for first stage study.

Private Schools

In 1997, 72 percent of students attended public-sector schools while 28 percent attended private institutions. There are two kinds of compulsory-level establishments that are not in the public sector: *centros concertados,* which are financed by public funds and account for approximately 90 percent of all private schools and *centros no concertados* which are totally private.

The *centros concertados* have many features in common with public schools such as cost-free education; teacher, parent and student participation in the control and management of the establishment and the admission system; non-profit extracurricular activities and services; and optional religious education. Private non-funded schools are free to establish their own internal rules, select teachers, establish admission procedures, lay down rules and regulations, and determine tuition fees.

Financing Education

Education is financed with public and private funds. Public funds are provided mainly by the MEC and by the Education Authorities in Autonomous Communities. Public spending is not only earmarked for public education, it is also allocated to finance student scholarships and grants and to subsidize private establishments.

In both compulsory and non-compulsory education, families have to pay for school materials and the textbooks, as well as for the use of services such as transportation and dining facilities.

Adult Education

Since 1990, the activity of the MEC is regulated by the LOGSE, thus putting it on the same footing as the other levels of education around which the systems are organized. Some of its objectives are to offer a basic education, which allows adults access to the different educational levels, to improve or get a professional qualification, and to develop their ability to participate in society, culture, politics and the economy. MEC provides minimal requirements, while the Autonomous Communities maintain responsibility for direct management.[4]

MEC finances some concrete activities organized by different public or private non-profit bodies, as well as the staff required for them. (See table 3.10.)

TABLE 3.10
Statistics on Adult Education

Number of establishments, other adult education actions, school year 1996–1997

Adult Education Establishments*	1,223
Other Adult Education Actions	653

Source: *Oficina de Planificacion y Estadistica. Ministerio de Educacion y Cultura*

Number of adult education teachers, school year 1996–1997

	Adult Education Teachers	Number of Women
Total	10,416	5,584
Civil servants	5,159	–
No civil servants	5,257	–

Source: *Oficina de Planificacion y Estadistica. Ministerio de Educacion y Cultura*

Number of pupils registered in adult education by academic area, school year 1996–1997

	Number of Pupils	% Women
Literacy	69,266	72.73
1st cycle	37,475	69.51
2nd cycle (*Certificado de Escolaridad*)	17,127	62.60
3rd cycle (*Graduado Escolar*)	121,356	50.48
Secondary education for adults	11,291	61.41
First tier vocational training for adults	44,797	81.54
Others	57,403	56.66

Source: *Oficina de Planificacion y Estadistica. Ministerio de Educacion y Cultura*

Total number of pupils older than twenty-five years of age enrolled in the several formative actions of the occupational vocational training at state level, 1997

Age of pupils	Female	Total
Older than 25	60,273	105,194

Source: *Ministerio de Trabajo y Asuntos Sociales*

Literacy Rates

Literacy rates in Spain are 98 percent for both men and women. The government recognizes that there is a need among Spaniards to further increase their literacy standing among the nations of the world. The number of functional illiterates in Spain is growing and there are stark contrasts in literacy in various regions of the country. To combat this problem, the government has launched a literacy campaign, and has increased adult education centers and continuing education programs. (See table A.1 in the appendix.)

School Enrollment Rates

The number of students enrolled at each level is a strong indicator of a country's educational level, social trends, and commitment to education. In Spain, in 1997 there are 2,567,012 students at the primary level, 3,852,102 at the secondary level, and 1,684,445 at the tertiary level. (See tables A.4, A.5, A.6, and A.7 in the appendix.)

Reforms of the Current Educational System

Spain is finishing a process of reform of its educational system. The enactment of the 1990 Organic Act on General Organization of the Educational System (LOGSE) as the basic legal text on education entailed the repeal of the 1970 law. A new structure and organization of the non-university education level will be implemented in the school year 2002-2003. The new model is a decentralized model that divides educational powers into those reserved to the State, those entrusted to the Autonomous Communities, and those commissioned to the municipal governments. The new Ministry of Education, Culture and Sport has changed its structure in order to play a leading role in the cooperation among Autonomous Communities, provide cohesion among various Autonomous Communities, and foster dialogue with all the Administrations, institutions and social agents in order to establish the basic rules for the educational system.

Additional reforms under consideration are: To extend cost-free education to six years; improve teaching of foreign languages, mathematics and Spanish languages in primary education, as well as to promote information and communication technologies; to strengthen common subjects and increase optional subject areas in secondary education; to strengthen those subjects corresponding to humanities in upper secondary education; and generally to improve the quality of vocational training.[5]

Notes

1. *Structure of Education, Initial Training, and Adult Education Systems in Europe, Spain 1999.* (Brussels: Eurydice European Unit).
2. Ibid.
3. Ibid.
4. Ibid.
5. Ibid.

Country Profiles: Eastern Europe

RUSSIAN FEDERATION

Background Information

The Russian Federation became an independent state in December 1991, as a result of the dissolution of the Union of Soviet Socialist Republics (USSR or Soviet Union). Russia was the largest and most prominent of the 15 republics of the Soviet Union until its dissolution in 1991.

Russia is the largest country in the world, with an area of 17,075,200 square kilometers (6,592,800 square miles). It constitutes more than one-ninth of the world's land area and is nearly twice the size of the United States or China. It encompasses eleven time zones and stretches across two continents, from Eastern Europe across northern Asia to the Pacific. Russia includes twenty-one republics; six territories known as krays; ten national areas called okrugs; forty-nine regions or oblasts; one autonomous oblast; and two cities with federal status.

Russia's population in 2000 was estimated at 145,904,542, making it the sixth most populous nation after China, India, the United States, Indonesia, and Brazil. Since the dissolution of the Soviet Union, Russia has seen an overall decline in its population despite the influx of immigrants from other parts of the former Soviet Union. Its population is unevenly distributed; the highest concentrations are found in European Russia.

Nearly three-fourths of all Russians reside in urban centers. Russia has one of the world's widest varieties of nationalities and ethnicities. There are over 120 nationalities present. The single largest group is Russian, constituting about 82 percent of the total population. Russian is the most commonly spoken language in business, government, and education. Since 1991, there have been over 100 different languages spoken in Russia. Some of the ethnic republics have declared official regional languages. The majority of Russian students are instructed in the Russian language and diplomas are only granted in Russian, Bashkir, and Tatar. Other non-Russian languages are taught to various degrees usually only for the first few years of schooling.

Since 1991, religious observance has increased and there has been a resurgence of traditional religions. Still, many Russian people are non-religious, believing in a combination of traditional beliefs and alternative beliefs such as witchcraft or astrology. About one-fourth of the population belongs to the Russian Orthodox Church. Muslims are the second largest religious denomination in Russia. There are also small minorities of other Christian denominations, as well as Buddhists, and Jews.

Structure of Government

Since independence, Russia has adopted a new constitution and system of government. Russia is a federal republic governed under a Constitution that took effect in 1993. The central government is composed of three independent branches: the executive (the president and the prime minister); the legislative (the Federal Assembly—consisting of the upper house, the Council of Federations, and the lower house, the State Duma); and the judiciary. The executive branch is considerably more powerful than the other two branches.

After the collapse of the Soviet Union, Russia began transforming itself into a more democratic society with an economy based on market mechanisms and principles. Russia has made many successful changes: there have been free elections at all levels of government, private ownership of property has been legalized, and large segments of the economy are now privately owned.[1]

But the transformation is far from complete. In the economic sphere, privatized assets have not been allocated fairly among the population and privatization of land is still in its infancy. Russia must also deal with the large-scale environmental destruction and other problems inherited from the Soviet Union. In the political sphere, a state society based on citizen involvement in local, regional, and national affairs has yet to develop.[2]

History of the Educational System

During the Soviet period, the government firmly controlled the education system. Schools emphasized skill building and taught children Communist ideology. Teachers were expected to shape their student's personalities to conform to Communist beliefs and ideology. The government controlled school activities. It issued textbooks and approved the lessons that were to be taught. Private schools were prohibited.

Basis of the Educational System—Principles and Legislation

The political developments that resulted in the breakup of the Soviet Union between August and December of 1991 and the establishment of an independent Russian Republic could not fail to be reflected in the Russian educational system. A comprehensive educational law, containing broad guarantees of educational freedom and of support for non-government schools was enacted in March 1992 and, with some revisions went into effect in August 1992. The new law reflects a very different spirit from the one enacted in 1984, which was widely perceived as having been written "by the bureaucrats for the bureaucrats: and thus incapable of stimulating real reform."[3]

The Constitution of the Russian federation provides the essential legal framework for education not only because it establishes a constitutional order that limits the centralizing traditions of the Soviet states, but also because it guarantees fundamental human rights and freedoms. Under Article 57, the Constitution guarantees free education. The Constitution provides that education is a fundamental right, "regardless of race, nationality, language, sex, age, health, social status, means, profession, descent, place of residence, religion, beliefs, party membership, criminal record" (Article 5(1)).

Control of the Educational System

The process of decentralization remains unresolved. The ambiguity before the breakup continues to exist in the federation. While transfer of functions from central to local government may seem a step towards democracy, it has become increasingly clear that the local authority can in fact be even more intrusive than a distant national authority.

Structure of the Educational System

Russia inherited a well-developed, comprehensive system of education from the Soviet period with an extensive network of preschool, elementary, secondary, and higher education.

Pre-primary Education

Enrollment in preschools, which is not obligatory, has dropped since the Soviet period, as tuition became more expensive. At this level, children learn basic skills that will help in their elementary education.

Compulsory Education

The Russian educational system is compulsory for both girls and boys through secondary school. It starts when a child reaches the age of six. Children enter primary school for a developmental course of study from grades one to four. Intermediate or secondary education is more intense and starts with grade five and continues through grade nine. (See table A.3 in the appendix.)

Post-compulsory Education

Children can enter upper-level schools or vocational technical programs, which include on-the-job training, after compulsory education is completed.

Higher Education

Higher education has undergone considerable transformation since 1991. Private schools have opened, some of which are operated by religious organizations others which are not. Public institutes of higher learning once heavily reliant on government funds now have to cover a more substantial amount of operating costs. Undergraduate training in higher educational institutions generally involves a four- to five-year course of study, after which a student may enroll in a one- to three-year program of graduate training. Graduate students who successfully complete their courses of study, comprehensive examinations, and the defense of their dissertation receive candidates of science degrees, which are roughly equivalent to doctoral degrees in the United States. A higher degree, the doctoral degree, is awarded to established scholars who have made outstanding contributions to their discipline. In the mid-1990s, about 4.5 million students were enrolled in Russian institutions of higher education.

Public and Private Schools

Whether public or private, individual schools have to be accredited by the government as to curriculum and qualifications.

All types of schools—government, private, or church-run—are allowed to have their own bank accounts and are encouraged to supplement their public funds to provide additional education services and activities.

In 1991, the government provided parents with a choice of various secondary and primary schools, for all income levels, in an attempt to establish free market education. These reforms were expected to stimulate school improvement, give parents more control over their child's education, and allow teachers to select schools that matched their own interests and skills. Some observers were concerned, however, that the advent of private schools catering to the rich would contribute to increased social class distinctions in Russian society.[4]

Financing Education

The Russian Constitution provides guaranteed access to free education (Article 57). But views on this issue have been changing over the past decade, as a result of a 1990 interview with the then-chairman of the USSR Supreme Subcommittee on Public Education, who said, "I don't think that paid education as such is so objectionable, if the fees are reasonable. It is even a good thing. And paid education means additional funds."

Schools that continue to be a part of the public system are subject to the provisions of the new education law guaranteeing "free general education" (Article 5(3)), and thus should not charge tuition. But some schools find ways to get around this. Parents may be asked to be a "sponsor" of the schools, or to provide funds in a variety of other ways.

Independent schools, by contrast, may charge any amount of tuition that the market will bear over and above funding received from government, which is at the same level as government schools.

Adult Education

After the Russian Revolution in 1917, the Soviet government virtually eliminated illiteracy through the establishment of various institutions and extension classes for adults. Since then, the Russian government has launched various programs similar to those during the Soviet regime to help combat illiteracy.

Alternative Forms of Education

In 1992, Russia adopted a new education law legalizing private schools and home schooling. This law also gave parents freedom to choose the type of school they wished their child to be enrolled in, as well as other aspects of their education.

Literacy Rates

Education in Russia advanced significantly during the Soviet period. In 1918, the Soviet government instituted free compulsory education, which enabled most Russians to receive a basic education. As a result, Russia has an extremely high literacy rate; it is among the highest in the world. More than 99 percent of both men and women over the age of fifteen are literate. (See table A.1 in the appendix.)

School Enrollment Rates

Enrollment varies from region to region. Primary enrollment ratios show that almost all children at this age level attend school, but at the secondary level it drops to 85 percent, and at the tertiary level it drops even further to 41 percent. (See tables A.4, A.5, A.6, and A.7 in the appendix.)

Reforms of the Current Educational System

Because of lack of space, students must attend school in shifts in one-third of Russia's schools. The physical conditions are repulsive. Many schools lack heating, plumbing, and other basic necessities. Thus, one major reform is reconstructing the school buildings for education.

Notes

1. "Russia," *Microsoft Encarta Encyclopedia Standard 2001*, CD–ROM. (Redmond, Wash.: Microsoft Corporation, 2001).
2. Ibid.
3. Charles L. Glenn. *Educational Freedom in Eastern Europe*. (Washington, D.C.: Cato Institute, 1997).
4. Ibid.

POLAND

Background Information

Poland is situated in Central Europe and covers 312,685 square kilometers. It is bordered on the north by the Baltic Sea and Russia; on the east by Lithuania, Belarus, and the Ukraine; on the south by the Czech Republic and Slovakia; and on the west by Germany. In 1997, Poland had a population of approximately 38.66 million, 62 percent of whom lived in urban areas and 38 percent in rural areas.

Communists ruled Poland from 1945 until 1989, when political and economic unrest resulted in the collapse of the regime. Poland is now run by a non-communist coalition.

In accordance with the Constitution, Poland is a Parliamentary Republic headed by the president of the Republic elected by direct popular vote for five years. The bicameral Parliament consists of 460 members in the lower chamber and 100 in the Senate. Members of the lower chamber and Senate are elected in general elections for four-year terms. The restoration of parliamentary democracy after 1989 has led to the emergence of numerous political parties.

Polish is the official language and is used by nearly all the population. The language contains a number of dialects, some of which are intermediate between Polish, German, and Ukrainian. The Polish language is written using the Latin alphabet and includes some letters that are additional to those used in English language. Some members of ethnic groups speak their own native languages in addition to Polish.

Poland is primarily Roman Catholic. Well over 90 percent of the people are Roman Catholic and Catholicism plays an important part in Poland's history and is a cornerstone of the country's identity. Other denominations represented in small numbers are Orthodox, Eastern Orthodox, and Evangelical Augsburg. A large number of Jehovah's Witnesses have arrived in Poland in recent years.

Basis of the Educational System—Principles and Legislation

The period of political transformation that started in 1989 brought about new legislation, which became the basis for changes in education. The new legislation permitted the development of non-state schools and changes in the structure of enrollment at the post-primary level as well as the doubling of the number of students attending institutions of higher education.[1]

The basic principles of the Polish education system are included in the Act on the Education System of September 7, 1991. Education is defined as part of "the common welfare of the whole society." It should be guided by the principles contained in the constitution and by instructions contained in universal, international legislative conventions.

The Act provides for the right of each Polish citizen to learn and the right of children and young people to be educated and cared for; the idea that schools support the family in shaping a child; the possibility for people of various ethnicities to establish and run schools and institutions; the adjustments of the content, method, and organization of education to pupils' psychophysical abilities; the possibility for students to get psychological care and special forms of didactic work; and the possibility for disabled and maladjusted children to learn at all types of schools.[2]

Control of the Educational System

The minister of education exercises control over the current educational policy. Almost all students, 99 percent, attend public schools. Most of the funds come from the state budget. The administration and organization of financial resources by schools are the subject of consultation between the school and the body running the school, i.e., local authorities (*gminy*) and district authorities (*powiats*).

The administration of education is decentralized. The responsibility for the administration of public nursery and primary schools has been delegated to local authorities (local communes). It has become the statutory responsibility of *powaits* (districts) to administer secondary schools, artistic, and special schools. The provinces (*viodships*) coordinate, supervise, and implement the policies of the Ministry of Education and are responsible for pedagogical supervision.[3]

Organization of the Educational System

Children aged three to six may attend pre-primary schools, but it is not compulsory. At the age of six most children attend kindergartens or other forms of pre-primary classes. Compulsory education starts at the age of seven and lasts until the age of sixteen.

Compulsory education is divided into primary education, lower secondary education, and upper education, including specialized secondary schools and vocational schools. The next level in the education system is the post-secondary school level in which a student attains higher education in universities, vocational schools, or post-secondary schools. After completion of higher education at the university level, students may continue for their masters and doctorate degrees.

Pre-primary Education

Pre-primary education is regarded as the first level of the school system. A child aged three to six may attend pre-primary school but it is not compulsory. The majority of six-year-olds attend either kindergartens (*prezdszkola*) or other forms of pre-primary classes (*oddzialy prezedskoine*). Six-year-old children also have a right to complete a year of preparation for primary education under municipal supervision. As many as 97.5 percent of children of this age take advantage of the provision.

Compulsory Education

As of school year 1999–2000, the Full-Time Compulsory Education Act states that when children reach the age of seven compulsory education begins and does not end until they are sixteen years of age. It covers education in six-year primary schools (*szkola podstawowa*) and three-year lower secondary schools (*gymnasia*). (See table A.3 in the appendix.)

Reformed six-year primary school (*Szkola podstawowa*)	seven to thirteen years of age Stage 1: integrated teaching, seven to ten years of age Stage 2: block teaching, ten to thirteen years of age
Three-year lower secondary school (*Gimnazjum*)	thirteen to sixteen years of age Stage 3: subject teaching

Primary School

The general objectives of the reformed six-year primary school are laid out by the minister of National Education in the regulations on Core Curriculum for General Education. They refer to three main educational dimensions: knowledge, skills, and moral development. The combination of all three is stressed.

Education in the new six-year primary school is divided into two stages:

Stage 1 (grades one to three), called integrated teaching, which is meant to provide a smooth transition from pre-primary education to primary school education. Educational activities are conducted according to a timetable prepared by the teacher in which the pupil's activity determines the duration of the lessons. Stage 2 (grades four to six), called block teaching, is arranged in blocks of subjects: natural sciences, humanities, and technology. The following subjects are excluded from block teaching: mathematics, physical education, and religion/ethics.[4]

Lower Secondary Education

The only admission requirement for lower secondary education is successful completion of six-year primary schooling and a primary school leaving certificate. Lower secondary school aims to arouse individual interests, introduce the pupils to the world of art, develop social skills, and introduce the pupils to the world of science by means of teaching language, concepts, theories, and methodologies specific to a given discipline. The organization of these schools is much the same as that of the primary system.

The Ministry decides curricula and assessments are made through a series of tests and final examinations. A certificate is needed from lower secondary schools to apply for higher education.

Upper Secondary and Post-secondary Education

At the upper secondary and post-secondary level, students can continue on with their education and specialize by choosing a specific discipline or attending vocational schools, which will prepare them for the workforce. The schools, except vocational schools, organize entrance exams to select students according to their knowledge and skills.

Higher Education

There are various types of non-university and university higher education institutions: *wyzsze szkoly zawodowe* (non-university higher vocational colleges), *kolegia nauczycielskie* (teacher training colleges), *uniwersytety* (traditional universities), *politechniki* (technological universities), and *akademie* (academies).

At the end of three- or four-year higher vocational education, students are awarded the vocational qualification diploma and the title of *licencjat* or *inzyeir*, which gives them access to the job market or to go on to higher studies. Universities and other university-type institutes of four-one-and-a-half to six-year duration issue *dyplom ukonczenia studiow wyzszych* (the university higher-education diploma). Students are awarded the title of *magister*, *magister injynier*, or *lekarz*, depending on the fields of studies they have followed. Students can then apply for a doctorate.

Private Schools

Pursuant to the Education Act of 1991, schools can be of two types: public schools, which offer free education within the framework of the core curriculum, and non-public schools. The latter can be civil (social), church, or private schools. All non-public schools may have their own curriculum, which are approved by the Ministry of Education. Non-public schools are financed by parents, private enterprises and foundations.

In the 1997–1998 school year, Poland had 363 non-public primary schools (136 private, 27 church, and 200 civic), 366 non-public general secondary schools (137 private, fifty-four church, and 165 civic), and 265 non-public vocational secondary and basic vocational schools—984 non-public schools altogether.

Less than one percent (0.7 percent) of students attend non-public primary schools. About 4.6 percent attend non-public general secondary school and about 1.9 percent attend non-public vocational secondary schools.

Financing Education

All educational tasks carried out by the three levels of local government are financed within the framework of a general subsidy from the State budget. The only exception is artistic education, which is still under control of the Ministry of Culture and National Heritage. The Ministry of Finance is responsible for the financing of the school system in Poland, including adult schools.

The Polish Constitution guarantees that higher education is free in full-time public schools. But there are exceptions. For example, charging fees is permitted in the case of courses being repeated due to unsatisfactory achievements and students who are applying for admission must pay an admission fee charge for an entrance exam.[5]

Adult Education

The Ministry of National Education is responsible for the coordination of adult education. In 1998, a separate division for continuing education and vocational education was established. The newly created division is responsible for adult education, excluding higher-education institutions. It is responsible for the organization of these schools as well as their effectiveness, and for the training of the staff. There are many levels of adult education ranging from teaching basic language and math skills to preparation for professional careers.

Literacy Rates

Education occupies an important position in Polish society, and virtually the entire population aged fifteen years and older is able to read and write. Poland's literacy rate stands in the ninety-ninth percentile for both men and women. (See table A.1 in the appendix.)

School Enrollment Rates

Approximately 3,021,378 children in Poland are enrolled at the primary level, but at the secondary level the numbers drop to 2,539,138, and at the tertiary level the numbers drop to 720,267. Reasons for the decline might be distance from school, economic necessity of work, or the lack of funds to continue education. (See tables A.4, A.5, A.6, and A.7 in the appendix.)

Reforms in Current Educational System

Poland is undergoing major reforms in its educational system. A new evaluation system will implement external standardized tests and examinations after completion of every level of education. Poland is hoping to assure better quality control in education, to support student's achievements, and to enable comparisons at a national level. Also, by the 2004–2005 school year, the general organization of the educational system will be altered yet again.

Notes

1. *Structures of Education, Initial Training and Adult Education Systems in Europe, Poland 1999.* (Brussels: Eurydice European Unit).
2. Ibid.
3. Ibid.
4. Ibid.
5. Ibid.

Country Profiles: Africa

SOUTH AFRICA

Background Information

South Africa occupies the southernmost portion of the African continent, bordered on the north by Namibia, Botswana, Zimbabwe, Mozam-
bique, and Swaziland; on the east and south by the Indian Ocean; and on
the west by the Atlantic Ocean.

Black Africans comprise three-fourths of South Africa's population,
and whites, coloreds (people of mixed race), and Asians (mainly Indians)
make up the remainder of the 42.7 million people.

Until recently, whites dominated the majority of the population under
the political genre of racial segregation known as apartheid. Apartheid
ended in the early 1990s, but South Africa is still recovering from the racial
inequalities in political power, opportunity, and lifestyle. The end of
apartheid led to the lifting of trade sanctions against South Africa imposed
by the international community. It also led to a total reorganization of the
government, which since 1994, has been a nonracial democracy based on
majority rule.

South Africa is divided into nine provinces: Gauteng, Northern
Province, Mpumalanga, North-West Province, Free State, Eastern Cape,
Northern Cape, Western Cape, and KwaZulu-Natal.

Until apartheid ended in 1994, Afrikaans and English were official languages, although they represent the native languages of only 15 percent and 9 percent of the total population, respectively. Afrikaans is spoken not only by Afrikaners but also by 83 percent of colored people. English is the primary language of many whites, and is spoken by 95 percent of Asians. The 1994 Constitution added nine African languages to the list of recognized, official languages: Zulu, Xhosa, Sesotho sa Leboa (Northern Sotho or Pedi), Tswana, Sesotho (Southern Sotho), Tsonga, Venda, Ndebele, and Swati. Many blacks can speak two or more of these languages, in addition to English and Afrikaans. Together, these eleven languages are the primary languages of 98 percent of South Africans.

In practice, English retains a dominant position as the main medium of instruction in schools and most universities. Afrikaners pride themselves on their language and have struggled to keep it as a medium of instruction and resist any threat to exterminate it.

Of the four-fifths of South Africans who profess religious faith, 77 percent are Christians. The remaining 3 percent are Hindus (1.74 percent), Muslims (1.09 percent), and Jews (0.41 percent). There are also many independent African religions. Most people who claim no religious affiliation are African traditionalists. Their religion has a strong cultural base and rituals vary according to ethnic group.

History of Education

Educational inequality has a long history in South Africa. Under apartheid, the education system was racially structured with separate national departments for whites, coloreds, Asians, and blacks outside of the *bantustans* (homelands). Ten separate education departments were established within the *bantustans*. Although government spending on black education increased greatly in the late 1980s, at the end of the apartheid era in 1994, per capita expenditure for white students was still four times higher than expenditures for blacks. Spending on education for Asians and colored people was closer to spending for whites.[1]

During apartheid, many black teachers were poorly qualified, and there were more than twice as many students per teacher for blacks as for whites outside the bantustans. Black schools had fewer classrooms than white schools, shortages of textbooks were common, and few schools had science laboratories of any kind. As a result, only about 40 percent of black candidates passed matriculation (the qualification for completing secondary school, a minimum requirement for entrance to a university) in the early 1990s. This compared with pass rates of about 85 percent for Colored students and 95 percent for whites and Asians. At least 1.5 million school-age blacks were not in school in the early 1990s, and only about 1 percent of those who started school eventually passed matriculation examinations. Because of this and the fact that education was compulsory for whites and Indians until 1994, there are tremendous disparities among races in education especially since children of different races had to attend different schools.[2]

Basis of the Educational System—Principles and Legislation

Before the apartheid era came to an end during the early 1990s, South Africa began to address the crisis in education. The government released the Education Renewal Strategy in 1993. Discussions involving government officials, educators, parents, and students were initiated in the mid-1980s and were formalized in the 1990s when a single Ministry of Education was established.

Efforts to reform educational institutions have faced various challenges. The primary obstacle was the limited amount of resources available for expenditure on education. The facilities in predominantly white schools were far superior to facilities in schools in black areas; many African schools—especially in rural areas—lacked basic necessities such as heat, plumbing, and electricity, as well as more advanced facilities such as science laboratories. A shortage of basic classroom supplies in black schools was also common.

Teachers were often poorly trained, particularly in the rural schools. Many teachers in suburban school systems, who generally were the most qualified, were reluctant to move to rural areas. Efforts were accelerated to improve the teacher-training system: qualifications required for primary and secondary teachers as well as for teachers from the different racial groups were standardized. All teachers must now complete a full secondary course plus a three-year training course.

Thus, in the early post-apartheid period, class differences and geographic considerations began to become more of a characteristic of the social divisions in the schools. Improvement in the system depended largely on increased availability of resources for education, which in turn depended on a strong South African economy.

A shift to a more Afrocentric curriculum was an important element of South African educational reform during the late 1990s. The government and private investors developed new curricula in which racial stereotypes were eliminated and the African perspective of their history was emphasized. New approaches, including the use of oral histories, were introduced during the 1990s.

Organization and Control of the Educational System

The challenge of restructuring education in post-apartheid society is difficult. The new government created a unified education system eliminating racial distinctions. Merging fourteen education departments into one has been a major undertaking. Currently, only three out of five children with Standard 5 education (seven years of school) are actually literate. The government mandates ten years of compulsory, state-provided education for all, but this will take time to achieve. Progress was made in 1995, when for the first time, all six-year-olds were enrolled in first grade. The number of private schools, attended largely by whites, increased dramatically in the mid-1990s as public schools were integrated.

Compulsory Education

South Africa mandates ten years of compulsory education for girls and boys, starting with a year of preschool and extending until the age of sixteen. But because schooling was compulsory only for whites and Indians until 1994, colored children and non-white races are at a disadvantage compared to their white and Indian friends.

Some of the basic features of South African education continued into the post-apartheid period. The system is organized into four three-year cycles: junior primary, senior primary, junior secondary, and senior secondary. Because the first year of the junior secondary cycle is taken in the primary school, the primary and secondary units are seven and five years, respectively.

General high schools are predominantly academic but often offer an expansive range of courses. Specialized high schools, at the senior secondary level, offer technical, agricultural, commercial, art, and domestic science courses. Apprenticeship may begin after the first year of the senior secondary phase (grade ten). Attempts are now being made to form regional comprehensive schools. (See table A.3 in the appendix.)

Post-secondary Education

The tertiary level of South African education includes universities, *technikons* (successors to the colleges of advanced technical education, offering programs of one to six years in engineering and other technologies, management, and art), technical colleges and institutes, and colleges of education. Technical centers, industrial training centers, and adult education centers extend training to those who leave school. During the 1990s many black university students demanded reduced admission standards and increases in scholarships and faculty appointments for blacks.[3]

South Africa has a well-developed higher education system, which was also racially segregated until after apartheid. In 1995, there were 385,000 students attending twenty-one universities and 190,000 students attending *technikons* (technical or vocational institutes). About 37 percent of each group was white. The numbers of blacks in historically white universities grew rapidly after 1994, even in Afrikaans-language universities. Most black students, however, attend historically black universities, including the ten township campuses of Vista University that opened in the early 1980s.[4]

Private Schools

Private schools are primarily located in the northeast and in the Cape region. More than nine-tenths of white South African children and virtually all black children are in state schools. This is in large part due to the tuition fees that are attached to attending a private school.

Financing Education

The government's budget for 1996 allocated 23.9 percent of total expenditures to education, but massive inequalities in teacher qualifications, buildings, sports facilities, and equipment are hard to eradicate. This applies not only to racial inequalities but also to differences among urban and rural areas. Overall, it is estimated that at least 2,000 new schools must be built, 65,000 new classrooms equipped, 60,000 teachers educated and trained, and 50 million textbooks printed. For a country such as South Africa this is difficult. There has also been concern about the financial difficulties of the different states within South Africa based on their current educational systems and their needs.

Adult Education

Increasing emphasis has been placed on improving and expanding vocational–technical, adult, and non-formal programs of education. Such efforts have included churches, community centers, and various other organizations that have established adult learning courses offered in the evenings.

Literacy Rates

The overall literacy rate for both men and women is 70 percent, varying in some rural areas where it may drop to below 50 percent. Generally, literacy is highest among whites in urban areas and lowest among coloreds in rural regions. (See table A.1 in the appendix.)

School Enrollment Rates

Boys in South Africa tend to have a higher dropout rate than girls: 53 percent compared with 44 percent at the primary level, and 51 percent compared to 46 percent at the secondary level. Among female university students, nearly 50 percent are white, 33 percent African, 7 percent colored, and 6 percent Indian. Women make up 29 percent of those enrolled in *technikons,* or technical colleges. In postgraduate programs, women constitute 46 percent of honors students, 32 percent of master's students, and 24 percent of doctoral candidates. (See tables A.4, A.5, A.6, and A.7 in the appendix.)

Reforms in the Current Educational System

The independent African states face numerous problems in implementing an educational policy that will encourage economic and social development. Organizational and structural problems and economic and political problems cause tremendous conflicts and difficulties among students, teachers, policy makers, parents, and the government.

Notes

1. "South Africa," *Microsoft Encarta Encyclopedia Standard 2001*, CD–ROM/(Redmond, Wash.: Microsoft Corporation, 2001).
2. Ibid.
3. Ibid.
4. Naomi Neft and Ann D. Levine, *Where Women Stand An International Report on the Status of Women in 140 Countries, 1997–1998.* (New York: Random House, 1997).

NIGERIA

Background Information

Nigeria is located in western Africa, bounded by Cameroon to the east, Chad to the northeast, Niger to the north, Benin to the west, and the Atlantic Ocean to the south. Nigeria covers an area of 356,669 square miles. It is the most populated of Africa's countries, with 98.1 million inhabitants. The population is largely rural, and only about 15 percent live in cities.

Nigeria has a federal form of government and is divided into thirty-six states and a federal capital territory. Most Nigerians speak more than one language. English, the country's official language, is widely spoken, especially among educated individuals. In many Nigerian cities, standard English is spoken side by side with the "pidgin," or a mixture of English and local languages. About 400 native Nigerian languages have been identified, and some are threatened with extinction. The most common of the native languages are Hausa, Yoruba, and Igbo.

Nigeria is a secular state, but two main religions are widely practiced in the country: Christianity and Islam. Small proportions of the people have traditional religious beliefs indigenous to Africa, or are atheists.

History of Education

For generations before the arrival of Europeans, Nigerians taught their children informally about their culture, work, survival skills, and social activities. Formal education came early to West Africa most commonly in the form of Christian missionaries or Islamic schools. The primary goal of the Islamic schools was to teach Arabic and the Koran, the holy book of the faith and guiding principles. Christian missionaries taught Christian moral values and attempted to instill western cultural values.[1]

Basis of the Educational System

In 1976 free and universal elementary education was introduced (UPE). In 1979 there was a return to civilian rule and the promulgation of a constitution which guaranteed the right to free education at all levels "when practicable." (FRN 1979). Also in 1979, the students formed the National Association of Nigerian Students (NANS). In 1983, NANS launched a Charter of Demands in which the right to education as an immediate measure was demanded. The Charter also condemned the chronic underfunding of education, gerontocratic authoritarianism in the internal management of the universities, and the lack of autonomy from the government. In December 1983, major cutbacks on public expenditures were implemented. As a result, many schools closed at all levels of the educational system, or tuition fees were charged. In August 1985, however, the government stated that undergraduates would not be charged tuition fees. As post-graduate work was not financed, many universities raised fees by more than 150 percent. Since 1984, the right to education has been undermined more by macroeconomic policy than by direct intervention.[2]

Control of the Educational System

The Federal Ministry of Education sets national policy and coordinates the financing of the system. Each state has a ministry of education that manages its primary and secondary schools as well as its technical colleges. In some states, local school communities assume responsibility for managing their schools.

There are nationwide commissions established by law, which oversee primary, technical and nomadic education, colleges of education, and the universities. These commissions regulate standards, disburse funds, and are expected to act as a buffer between the institutions and government.

Both federal and state governments control secondary and higher education institutions, while local governments largely run primary schools. Often private individuals and organizations jointly run primary and secondary schools. There are also legal provisions for the establishment of private universities.

Organization of the Educational System

The Nigerian education system is based on the "6–3–3–4" model, meaning that students spend six years in primary school, three years in junior secondary school, three years in senior secondary school, and four years at the post-secondary level. Students going on to senior secondary school can choose between commercial, technical, or grammar disciplines. The staff, materials and technology are generally insufficient and thus deny the continuous flow of the education system.

Compulsory Education

Compulsory education consists of primary education and secondary education. Primary education is in need of reform. In a study conducted by Paul Francis of the World Bank, the school environment was found to be not conducive to learning, pupil safety, security, or health. Classroom space is inadequate and students have classes outside or attend classes with up to four other classes. Schools are in need of repair, but because of lack of funding they are unable to meet maintenance or upkeep costs, or to obtain educational supplies. Schools often lack offices, desks, furniture, recreational facilities, and have few or no toilets. Vocational education is organized at the secondary level.[3]

Post-secondary Education

Higher education in Nigeria is composed of colleges of education, colleges of technology, colleges of basic studies, polytechnics, schools of nursing, colleges of agriculture, and the universities. The conventional universities are differentiated according to areas of specialization: agriculture, technology, and general.

In 1996, Nigeria had thirty-seven universities—twenty-five funded by the federal government and twelve by state governments. The oldest, the University of Ibadan, was founded in 1948 as a college of the University of London and became autonomous in 1962. Since 1980 several more universities have opened, including institutes specializing in agriculture and technology. A variety of polytechnic schools, including Yaba College of Technology in Lagos and Kaduna Polytechnic, offer non-degree post-secondary programs. In 1994, the total enrollment in Nigerian universities was 208,000.[4]

The struggle for university autonomy and academic freedom in Nigeria is conditioned by economic deprivation as the result of corruption, political instability, military authoritarianism, and institutional overload and decay.

Financing Education

The state government funds education at the primary and secondary level. The national or state government funds university education. Most children attend public schools. Private schools require tuition fees.

Literacy Rates

Adult literacy is estimated to be 72 percent for men and 56 percent for women—an improvement over years past resulting from universal primary education and programs for adult literacy. A government commission was established in 1992 to combat illiteracy. Official data, however, estimate literacy only in English, thus discounting the significant level of literacy among northern Muslims. (See table A.1 in the appendix.)

School Enrollment Rates

By 1990, only 72 percent of children attended the compulsory first six years of education, due to government cutbacks, rising school fees, the deterioration of buildings, inferior instruction, and poor prospects for graduates. Enrollment rates remain lower for girls than boys, primarily because many rural northerners remain skeptical about schooling for girls. In 1996, the enrollment rate for secondary schools was 34 percent.

It is estimated that slightly more than half of all girls of primary school age are not in school, and of those who enroll, many drop out. Some localities have tried to reduce the number of dropouts by prohibiting parents from taking their daughters out of school.

Since independence came to the countries of West Africa the most impressive educational feature has been the rapid rate of expansion. During the past thirty years the number of students enrolled at all levels has more than quadrupled. Country after country has introduced some form of universal or compulsory primary education, built more secondary schools and opened at least one national university. This massive expansion has been made possible through the infusion of large sums of money by new governments who saw the quick expansion of educational opportunities as a political necessity.[5]

Regional imbalances in enrollment were found at the elementary level, with lower enrollment in the northern compared to the southern zones, particularly with respect to female students. Throughout Nigeria some 15 million children are enrolled in their 40,000 public primary schools. (See tables A.4, A.5, A.6, and A.7 in the appendix.)

Reforms in the Current Educational System

Various proposed reforms for the Nigerian educational system include lifting the ban on NANS, providing greater autonomy in higher education, providing more funding for education, improving facilities, instituting better reviewing processes and eliminating gender biases and gaps.

Notes

1. George E. F. Urch, *Education in Sub-Saharan Africa: A Source Book.* (New York: Garland, 1992).

2. *State of Academic Freedom in Africa 1995.* CODESRIA. Dakar, Senegal, (ISBN 2-86978-061-3).

3. Paul A. Francis, *Hard Lessons: Primary Schools Community and Social Capital in Nigeria.* (Washington, D.C., World Bank, 1998).

4. "Nigeria," *Microsoft Encarta Encyclopedia Standard 2001,* CD–ROM. (Redmond, Wash.: Microsoft Corporation, 2001).

5. Ibid.

Country Profiles: Middle East

IRAQ

Background Information

Iraq occupies the greater part of the ancient land of Mesopotamia. It is bound on the north by Turkey; on the east by Iran; on the south by Saudi Arabia, Kuwait, and the Persian Gulf; and on the west by Jordan and Syria. The country has an area of 167,925 square miles.

The total population of Iraq is approximately 21,800,000. About 75 percent are Arab. Kurds, inhabiting the highlands of northern Iraq, constitute about 15 to 20 percent of the population. In the rural areas of the country many people still live in tribal communities, leading a nomadic or semi-nomadic existence keeping herds of camels, horses, and sheep. The overall population density in 1997 was about fifty-one persons per square kilometer People tend to be concentrated near river systems. The population of Iraq is about 70 percent urban.

Iraq is divided into eighteen governorates, fifteen of which are headed by centrally appointed governors. The other three provinces, in the northeast, together constitute the Kurdish Autonomous Region, which established its own Kurdish National Assembly in 1992.

The principal executive organization of Iraq is the Revolutionary Command Council, which is led by a chairman. The council also selects a president. In practice, political power is centralized in a single leader who serves as the nation's president, as its Prime Minister, and as chairman of the Revolutionary Command Council. A council of ministers is the country's main administrative body.

A National Assembly was established in 1980. It is made up of 250 members popularly elected to four-year terms. The Revolutionary Command Council also has legislative functions.

The judicial system of Iraq allows for separate treatment of civil and religious matters. Civil matters are handled in courts presided over by individual judges. Above these courts are five courts of appeals, located in the major cities, and a court of annulment in Baghdad. Muslim courts usually handle religious matters.

Arabic is the official language of Iraq. Kurdish is the official language in the Kurdish Autonomous Region. Instruction for educational purposes is in Arabic, although Kurdish is used in primary schools in the Autonomous Region.

Approximately 95 percent of the people of Iraq are Muslims. About 60 to 65 percent of the Muslims adhere to the Shiite branch and the rest to the Sunnite branch. Among the few Christian sects in Iraq are the Nestorians, the Jacobite Christians, and offshoots of these two sects, respectively known as Chaldean and Syrian Catholics. In addition, smaller religious groups include the Yazidis, and a group known as the Mandaean Baptists. A small community of Jews lives in Baghdad.

Control of the Educational System

The Ministry of Education and the Ministry of Higher Education are responsible for education at all levels, although other ministries have some specific educational functions in their respective fields.

Organization of the Educational System

Education is divided among three primary levels of education. Primary education is a six-year cycle, secondary education is also a six-year cycle divided into three years of preparatory and secondary school, and the final level is higher education which consists of various technical and university facilities.

Compulsory Education

Education is compulsory for children ages six through fifteen, or for six years of primary education and the first three years of secondary preparatory school. But some children in rural areas do not attend schools because of inadequate facilities.

Primary school is a six-year cycle, which includes Arabic language, Islamic studies, arithmetic, art, music, and physical education. A final examination must be passed at the end of the sixth primary year in order to advance to the next level.

Secondary education is also a six-year cycle, divided into three years of preparatory and secondary school. At the end of the third preparatory year, students must pass an exam and receive the Preparatory Certificate in order to continue to the secondary level. Options at the secondary level include general secondary education in the scientific, literary, or commercial track, secondary vocational schools (including those for nursing and health), police training, and primary teacher training. Graduates from vocational training schools usually enter the workforce immediately after they complete their programs, although some may continue on to higher training or university studies. Upon completion of the third and final year of secondary education, students must pass a baccalaureate exam in order to qualify for university admission.[1]

Post-secondary Education

Post-secondary education is available at technical institutes as well as universities. Iraq has eight universities, four in Baghdad and one each in Basra, Irbil, Mosul, and Tikrit. The country also has eighteen technical institutes. Technical institutions include institutions of administration, agricultural applied arts, medicine and technology. All technical institutes require a secondary school certificate. They offer two-year programs, which result in the award of a diploma or certificate. The languages of instruction are English and Arabic. University admission requirements include a maximum age of twenty-four and a secondary school certificate or equivalent. The discipline students can pursue at the university level depends largely on their track in secondary school.

Financing Education

Public education in Iraq is free for all citizens. Private schools require some form of tuition fees. The federal government finances higher education at the university level.

Literacy Rates

About 58 percent of Iraqis over the age of fifteen are literate. There is a strong contrast between the rates for men and women. Men average 68 percent literacy while women are only 41 percent literate. The length of compulsory education in a country is a good indicator of the level of education in the country. In Iraq there is only six years of compulsory education. (See table A.1 in the appendix.)

School Enrollment Rates

In the early 1990s, about 3 million pupils attended elementary schools, and some 1.1 million students were enrolled in secondary schools. In addition, about 152,900 students attended vocational or teacher-training institutions. Approximately 197,800 students were enrolled in institutions of higher education. (See tables A.4, A.5, A.6, and A.7 in the appendix.)

Reforms in the Current Educational System

The Iraqi government is in the process of addressing reforms related to the quality of education and the illiteracy rates. Another goal of Iraqi education is to ensure that all citizens receive some form of education.

Note

1. *Education in the Middle East.* Leslie C. Schmida, ed. and Deborah G. Keenum. (Washington, D.C.: AMIDEAST, 1997).

EGYPT

Background Information

Egypt is located in northeastern Africa on the Mediterranean Sea and the southwestern portion of Asia. It is the most populous country in Africa after Nigeria. In 2000, the population of Egypt was estimated to be 58,519,000. Slightly more than half of Egyptians, 56 percent, live in rural regions.

Egypt is a presidential republic. Power is concentrated in the head of state, the president. The prime minister is appointed by the president and serves as the head of the government. The legislature is unicameral and consists of the People's Assembly.

Nearly the entire population of Egypt speaks Arabic. But only well-educated people easily understand standard Arabic. Colloquial Egyptian Arabic is the language of daily conversation. English and French are common second languages among educated Egyptians.

Islam is the official religion of Egypt, and its legal statutes are the primary source of the country's civil law. Nine out of ten Egyptians are Muslims; almost all of the remainder are Coptic Christians, the largest Christian minority in the Middle East.

With regard to women, Egypt is one of the Middle East's most liberal societies. But although the Egyptian Constitution grants equal rights for women and men, various cultural and religious traditions, as well as some aspects of the country's laws, create great inequalities. In many of the lower class rural areas, women are viewed as inferior. Women are required to wear traditional head covering in public, talk only to males in their family, and defer to senior male relatives. Wives cannot receive a passport without their husband's consent. A woman can only receive half the amount that her male counterpart receives when a family member dies.

Basis of the Educational System—Principles and Legislation

Egypt's educational system reflects the internal division of its own people—between traditions and innovations, and between foreign and national interests.

Control of the Educational System

A trend towards the decentralization of educational authority has been evident in Egypt for some time, with administrative control shifting to the governorate level. Each of Egypt's twenty-five governorates comprises an educational zone, where a local education council supervises general secondary, vocational, technical, and teacher training schools. Town education councils are responsible for supervising local preparatory and primary schools, and village education councils supervise primary schools at the village level. The Ministry of Education is responsible for making and implementing general education policies and has ultimate authority over all public and private schools through the secondary level. The Ministry of Higher Education assumes responsibility for Egypt's colleges and universities.[1]

Organization of the Educational System

The Egyptian government reorganized and combined the first nine years of education into what is called Basic Education. The goals are to prevent a "backsliding into illiteracy, and meaningful participation in practical life."[2]

Pre-primary Education

Pre-primary education is not compulsory in Egypt but most four-year-olds do attend. Children learn a variety of skills and habits that prepare them for further education.

Compulsory Education

Beginning in 1981, compulsory education was changed to a two-stage structure, consisting of a nine-year Basic Education Stage and a three-year Secondary Stage. In cities, schools are built to provide all nine grades of Basic Education in the same building. Compulsory education was extended to age fifteen rather than twelve. Egypt has free compulsory education for girls and boys ages six to fifteen. (See table A.3 in the appendix.)

Basic Education

Basic education is designed to develop basic literacy skills. Subjects taught at this level include religion, Arabic, mathematics, science, social studies, technical education, agriculture or home economics, physical education, and music. The higher level of basic education introduces the study of a European language—usually English.

Secondary Education

Students at the secondary level in Egypt may follow either the general secondary program or a technical secondary program. General secondary education is a three-year program consisting of grades ten through twelve. All students follow a generalized course of study during the first year and then choose to follow either literary (liberal arts) or a scientific track in the remaining two years.

Technical secondary education runs parallel to the general secondary system and comprises three years of study aimed at producing skilled workers in industrial, agricultural, and commercial fields. Admission requires the Preparatory School Certificate and an age of not more than eighteen years.[3]

Post-secondary Education

Post-secondary academic training is available in Egypt at intermediate higher institutions.

Intermediate higher institutions offer two-year post-secondary programs and include teacher training institutes as well as vocational training institutes responsible to the Ministry of Education. Many higher education institutions have been integrated into the university system since 1975.

Universities in Egypt are centralized and competitive. All those holding the GSEC may enter Faculties of Commerce, Archeology, Mass Communications, Language, Economics, and Political Science. Literary Division graduates may also enter the Faculties of Law and Arts; scientific graduates may apply to the additional Faculties of Science, Engineering, Medicine, Agriculture, Dentistry, Pharmacy, and Nursing.

In 1962, education was made free up to the doctoral level and since then enrollment has increased tremendously in all higher education institutions. The government maintains a policy of employing all college graduates who cannot locate acceptable private sector employment within one year after graduation, which helps attract many university applicants. The government has trouble accommodating this high demand for university education, which results in overcrowding, lack of adequate faculty supervision, and limited post-graduate career prospects.

Egypt's universities as well as some of the higher institutes offer bachelors, masters, and doctoral degrees in addition to diplomas in special subjects.[4]

Private Schools

Most schools are state-run public schools. In recent years, private or religiously-affiliated schools have had increasing enrollment rates.

Financing Education

Since 1923, primary and intermediate education has been free, and it is now compulsory for children between the ages of six and fifteen. Public secondary and university education is also free but is not compulsory. The American University in Cairo (1919) is the only private and fee-charging institution of higher education.

Adult Education

In 1960, Egypt established a "schools for the people" system designed to educate the adult population. Adults are taught classes in basic literacy up to advanced technical programs.

Alternative Forms of Education

At the University level, enrollment is incredibly high. To help accommodate all the students, the government has instituted external education. In many cases, external students are those who are unable to qualify for formal enrollment, but in certain subjects they may study at home and, for a fee, sit for the final exams each year. While this opens the doors of higher education to many more students, it often reduces the quality of education and tends to stimulate enrollment in fields where an excess of graduates already exists.

Literacy Rates

While adult literacy rates have been rising over the past several decades, the literacy rate for women, at 41 percent, is still one of the lowest in the Middle East. Although more than half of women under forty-five can read and write, only 15 percent of women aged forty-five to sixty-four are literate, and among women over sixty-five, only 6 percent are literate.

In 2000, 55.3 percent of the adult population was literate—66.6 percent of males and 43.7 percent of females. (See table A.1 in the appendix.)

School Enrollment Rates

Employment and job training discourage children from remaining in school. Furthermore, many Islamic parents withdraw their daughters from school when they reach puberty because Egyptian men, especially among the lower class, prefer to marry women who have followed the custom of *purdah*—keeping girls and women secluded in their homes.

The percentage of girls enrolled in primary school has been increasing gradually, from 58 percent in 1980 to 86 percent in 1990. Although girls are still outnumbered by boys at every level, graduation rates are the same for both sexes.

Rapid population growth has severely overburdened Egypt's educational system. Classrooms from the primary school level to the university level are overcrowded, and schools lack many resources—such as up-to-date science laboratories, audiovisual aids, and even sufficient numbers of desks and textbooks. Although primary school enrollment is officially 100 percent, many children attend school irregularly or not at all because they must work to help support their families. (See tables A.4, A.5, A.6, and A.7 in the appendix.)

Reforms in the Current Educational System

Proposed reforms in the Egyptian educational system are numerous. Of primary concern is the government's effort to decentralize the educational authority and to eradicate illiteracy.

Notes

1. *Education in the Middle East.* Leslie C. Schmida, ed. and Deborah G. Keenum. (Washington, D.C.: AMIDEAST, 1997).

2. Ibid.

3. Ibid.

4. Ibid.

ISRAEL

Background Information

Israel is a small Middle Eastern country located on the eastern end of the Mediterranean Sea. It is bounded by Lebanon on the north, Syria on the northeast, Jordan on the east and by Egypt on the southwest. Its southernmost tip extends to the Gulf of Aqaba, which is part of the Red Sea. Israel's position as the center of Judaism surrounded by Arab and predominantly Islamic countries has influenced nearly every aspect of its foreign relations, demography, and economic policy throughout its history.

Between 1948 and the late 1990s, Israel had absorbed 2.1 million immigrants—four times the Jewish population before independence. In 2000, the population was estimated to be 5,851,913. Jews make up 82 percent of the population, and Arabs make up almost the entire remainder.

Israel is a multiparty parliamentary republic with ultimate authority vested in the legislature, or Knesset. There is no written constitution, but a number of basic laws passed by the parliament over the decades determine government operations and activities. Israel has a unitary, or non-federalist, system of government and the central government in Jerusalem runs most government functions.

Hebrew and Arabic are the official languages of Israel. The Jewish majority speaks a contemporary derivative of the Hebrew language, a biblical Semitic language. Immigrants are given intensive instruction in Hebrew, but many continue to speak their native language at home. Israeli Arabs speak Arabic. Both Hebrew and Arabic are taught in schools and used in legal matters and in the legislature. Many Israelis speak English, Russian, or a number of other combinations of European languages.

For centuries, this region has been the center for three major world religions: Judaism, Christianity, and Islam. About three-fourths of Israel's non-Jewish population follows Sunni Islam. Most of the remainder are Christians or Druze, a distinct religious minority. The largest Christian denominations are Greek Catholic and Greek Orthodox, although many other Christian denominations are also represented in Israel. Religious affiliation remains very important socially and politically. Israeli law guarantees religious freedom.

Basis of the Educational System—Principles and Legislation

The Compulsory Education Law of 1949 and subsequent amendments guarantee free and compulsory schooling for children ages five to sixteen and additional free, but not compulsory education, until the age of eighteen.

A major change occurred in 1968 with the Reform Act, which changed the schooling structure from a two-level system: Primary (kindergarten through grade eight) and secondary (grades nine through twelve) to a three-tier system: elementary (kindergarten through grade six), intermediate (grades seven through nine), and secondary (grades ten through twelve). The main goals of this reform were to raise the academic achievements of all students and to foster social integration. The reform has been implemented in about 55 to 60 percent of Israeli schools.

Control of the Educational System

The Ministry of Education is responsible for developing school curricula, educational standards, supervising teaching personnel and constructing school buildings. Local authorities are responsible for school maintenance and the acquisition of equipment and supplies. Teaching personnel at the kindergarten and primary school levels are Ministry employees, while those in the higher grades are employed by local authorities, which receive funding from the Ministry according to the number of students. Three main administrative bodies are maintained by the Council for Higher Education which controls higher education.

Organization of the Educational System

The state education system is split between a two-tier and three-tier schooling structure. Formal education begins in primary school (grades one through six) and continues with intermediate school (grades seven through nine) and secondary school (grades ten through twelve).

Pre-primary Education

The goal of pre-primary education is to have children further develop their social and language skills. The curricula of all preschools are guided and supervised by the Ministry of Education to ensure a solid and well-rounded foundation for future learning. Many two-year-olds and almost all three- and four-year-olds attend some kind of preschool institution. Local authorities sponsor most programs; others are privately owned. The Ministry of Education allocates special resources for preschool education in disadvantaged areas.

Compulsory Education

School attendance is obligatory from ages six to sixteen and free until age eighteen. Compulsory education consists of both primary and secondary education. (See table A.3 in the appendix.)

Primary Education

Primary school is from grades one through six. Schools systems may choose a variety of study materials provided by the Ministry of Education, which best suits their school. Compulsory academic studies are universal among schools with the aim of enhancing a student's understanding of their society. Each year a special topic of national importance is studied in depth. Past themes have included democratic values, the Hebrew language, immigration, Jerusalem, peace, and industry.

Secondary Education

The majority of secondary schools offer full academic curricula in science and in the humanities leading to a matriculation certificate and higher education. Other secondary schools offer more specialized curricula, which also leads to a certificate and/or vocational diploma.

Technological schools train technicians and practical engineers on three levels, with some preparing for higher education, some studying towards a vocational diploma, and others acquiring practical skills. Agricultural schools supplement basic studies with subjects relating to agronomy. Military preparatory schools, in two different settings, train future career personnel and technicians in specific fields required by the Israel Defense Forces. Both programs are residential, one is open to boys only, the other is coeducational. Yeshiva high schools, mainly boarding schools, with separate frameworks for boys and girls, complement their secular curricula with intensive religious studies and promote observance of tradition as well as a Jewish way of life. Comprehensive schools offer studies in a variety of vocations, ranging from bookkeeping to mechanics, electronics, hotel trades, graphic design, and more.

The Ministry of Labor provides apprenticeship programs in schools affiliated with vocational networks. Lasting three to four years, these programs consist of two years of classroom study followed by one or two years during which students study three days a week and work at their chosen trade on the other days. Trades range from hair styling and cooking, to mechanics and word processing.

Post-secondary Education

Higher education in Israel usually follows twelve years of primary and secondary education. The only prerequisite to attend any form of post-secondary institution is a certificate (*bagrut*) or its equivalent. Some fields of study require minimum grades in examinations. Most institutions require candidates to submit psychometric entrance examination scores. The only requirement for the Open University is that applicants be capable of academic study.

Pre-academic preparatory programs have been set up in universities, teacher training colleges, and regional colleges to provide a second chance to enter higher education to individuals who did not obtain a matriculation certificate at the culmination of their secondary level education or who want to improve their chances of being accepted in an institution of higher education. The duration of the programs provided by universities is one year (except for special cases) while programs administered by regional colleges and teacher training colleges can run for as long as two, and in some cases, three years.

Post-secondary educational opportunities include universities as well as vocational and other adult education programs. Most students complete compulsory military service—three years for men and two years for women—before advancing to higher education. The higher education system includes universities, non-university institutions of higher education that provide instruction at the bachelor's degree level only, regional colleges that offer academic courses under the academic responsibility of the universities, and non-academic post-secondary schools. All of these institutions are characterized by complete freedom in academic affairs.

Universities, which operate under the authority of the Council for Higher Education, include the Technion-Israel Institute of Technology in Haifa; the Hebrew University of Jerusalem; Bar-Ilan University in Ramat Gan; and Tel Aviv University, Haifa University, and Ben Gurion University of the Negev in Beersheba.

The Open University of Israel, established in 1974 in Tel Aviv-Yafo, allows students to learn through distance education and other forms of self-study. Other forms of adult education are especially important in Israel due to the high number of adult immigrants with varying levels of education in their home countries. Vocational and adult education subjects include nursing, teacher training, Hebrew language, art, music, and architecture.

The duration of studies for a bachelor's degree in universities depends on the discipline studied. Most disciplines require three years of study.

Private Schools

The multicultural nature of Israel is apparent within the education system. Accordingly, schools are divided into four groups: state schools, attended by the majority of students; state religious schools, which emphasize Jewish studies, tradition and observance; Arab and Druze schools, with instruction in Arabic and special focus on Arab and Druze history, religion and culture; and private schools, which operate under various religious and international auspices. In recent years, with the growing concern of parents over the orientation of their children's education, some new schools have been founded, which reflect the philosophies and beliefs of specific groups of parents and educators. About 10 percent of the school population aged thirteen to eighteen attend boarding schools.

Some secondary schools specialize in technological, agricultural, military, or religious studies. There are also private religious schools affiliated with ultra-Orthodox groups and Christian denominations.

Financing Education

The government finances 72 percent of education, while the rest comes from local authorities and other sources. Students often rely on government aid to finance their education.

Adult Education

The rapid expansion of adult education reflects the challenges facing the education system. A wide range of courses sponsored by the Ministry of Education, as well as by public and private institutions, address individual needs ranging from learning the Hebrew language and upgrading basic educational skills to promoting family well being and expanding general knowledge. The Ministry of Labor provides vocational training and retraining for adults in many fields. Most programs are available in the large cities, as well as in many towns. All in all, adult education as a leisure activity is becoming increasingly popular in Israel, especially among senior citizens.

Literacy Rates

The quality of Israel's education system and the high literacy rate of its people reflect the importance of education in the Jewish tradition. Men have a literacy rate of 95 percent and women of 89 percent. (See tables A.1, A.4, A.5, A.6, and A.7 in the appendix.)

School Enrollment Rates

In practice, about 90 percent of school-age children complete compulsory education. At present, well over half of Israelis in the twenty to twenty-four age group are enrolled in one of the country's institutions of post-secondary or higher education.

Reforms in the Current Educational System

Current reforms and changes in Israeli educational system include reorganizing the structure of the system, changing curricula policies, patterns of matriculation, and educational policymaking. The goal is continuing excellence and equality in education.

Plans for the future include expanding Israel's network of non-university higher education and including more direct state control.

Country Profiles: Asia

INDIA

Background Information

India is located in southern Asia. It is bound on the north by Afghanistan, China, Nepal and Bhuta, on the east by Bangladesh, Myanmar, and the Bay of Bengal; on the south by the Palk Strait, the Gulf of Mannar and the Indian Ocean; and on the west by the Arabian Sea and Pakistan. It is the world's seventh largest country in area. India occupies more than three million square kilometers. With more than one billion inhabitants, India ranks second only to China among the world's most populous countries. It is home to 16 percent of the world's population. India is divided into twenty-six states and six union territories.

India has had a federal political system and democratic government for more than fifty years. The country is a member of the Commonwealth of Nations, an association of political entities that once gave or currently give allegiance to the British monarchy. India is a federal republic, governed under a constitution and incorporating various features of the constitutional systems of the United Kingdom, the United States, and other democracies. The powers of the government are separated into three branches: executive, legislative, and a judiciary headed by a Supreme Court. Like the United States, India is a union of states, but its federalism is slightly different. The central government has power over the states, including the power to redraw state boundaries. But the states, many of which have large populations sharing a common language, culture and history, have an identity that is in some ways more significant than that of the country as a whole.

Although the Indian Constitution grants equal rights, strong patriarchal traditions persist, and women's lives continue to be shaped by centuries-old customs and classifications: caste, class, region, ethnicity, and religion. In most Indian families a daughter is viewed as a burden, and from early childhood a girl is often conditioned to believe that she is inferior and subordinate to men. In rural areas, parents often dismiss their daughter's education because she will soon be married and live with her in-laws.

The challenges of educational development in India can only be understood against the background of the great diversity in educational and socioeconomic status among the states. Three-fourths of children who are not enrolled in school live in six states—Andhra Pradesh, Bihar, Madhya Pradesh, Rajasthan, Uttar Pradesh, and West Bengal. The financial burden of providing good quality education to all children therefore falls disproportionately on these six states. Moreover, many of the children who do not attend school live in remote areas, belong to underprivileged groups, or have special educational needs.

English is spoken by as many as five percent of Indians, and various Dravidan languages are spoken by about 25 percent. Hindi is the language of the majority of the people. Many Indians speak more than one language, especially those who live near state borders or cities. The many languages and dialects are politically and socially significant. Eighteen major languages and more than 1,000 minor languages and dialects are spoken in India.

Religion has deep historical roots and is important in the life of the country. Hinduism and Buddhism both originated in India. Most people in India practice Hinduism (83 percent) with Islam a distant second (11 percent). Other practiced religions include Christianity (2 percent), Sikhism (2 percent), Buddhism (0.7 percent), and Jainism (0.4 percent). Most Indians live in rural areas and only about one-quarter of the population live in urban areas.

Basis of the Educational System—Principles and Legislation

Educational policy and progress are reviewed on a continual basis to reflect the goals of national development and priorities at a given time.

India's commitment to the spread of knowledge and freedom of thought among its citizens is reflected in its Constitution. The Directive Principle contained in Article 45 mandates that "the State shall endeavor to provide within a period of ten years from the commencement of this Constitution, for free and compulsory education for all children until they complete the age of fourteen years."

Although education is recognized in the Constitution, the State governments are an integral part of the development of education, particularly at the primary and the secondary level.

Control of the Educational System

The origin of the Indian Education Department dates back to pre-Independence when, for the first time, a separate Department was created in 1910 to supervise education. But soon after India achieved its independence on August 15, 1947, a full-fledged Ministry of Education was established on August 29 of that year. The responsibilities of the Education Department have undergone changes since the time of Independence. At present, the Ministry has three departments: the Department of Secondary Education and Higher Education, the Department of Elementary Education and Literacy; and the Department of Women and Child Development.

State governments control their own school systems, with some assistance from the central government. The Federal Ministry of Education directs the school systems of centrally administered areas, provides financial help for the nation's institutions of higher learning, and handles tasks such as commissioning textbooks.

Organization of the Educational System

Education generally consists of ten years of elementary and high school, two years of higher secondary education, and three years at the university level. (See table A.3 in the appendix.)

Students begin specializing in subjects in higher secondary school. A university typically has one or more colleges of law, medicine, engineering, and commerce, and many have colleges of agriculture. Prestigious and highly selective institutes of management have also been established. The educational establishment also includes a number of high-level scientific and social science institutes, as well as academies devoted to the arts.

Pre-primary Education

Pre-primary education in India is not compulsory. Children may attend until they reach the age of five. In pre-primary education the aim is the development of social and developmental skills.

Compulsory Education

Education is compulsory in India from the ages of six to fourteen. Primary schools are often in non-formal centers, as well as in upper primary schools.

Since Independence, the central and state governments have been expanding the provisions of primary formal and non-formal education to realize the goal of Universalization of Elementary Education (UEE). The challenge now is to sustain and deepen current reforms in education and encourage local planning and management of strategies for expanding and improving primary education.

The Kasturba Gandhi Shiksha Yojana, a program to establish residential schools for girls in all districts due to the low female literacy rate, has recently been announced. A sum of Rs. 2,500 million has been provided in the 1999 budget for this project. The central government has also decided to grant financial incentives and scholarships for girls born to families living below the poverty line to ensure that they receive a basic education.

Secondary Education

Secondary education serves as a bridge between primary and higher education. It is expected to prepare students between the ages of fourteen and eighteen for both work and the entry into higher education. Secondary Education starts with classes nine to ten leading to higher secondary classes from eleven to twelve. The relevant population at the secondary and senior secondary level as projected in the 1996–1997 school year by NSSO has been estimated at 9.66 *crores* (a *crore* is 10,000,000). Against this population, the enrollment figures for 1997–1998 shows that only 2.70 *crores* are attending schools. Thus, two-thirds of the eligible population remains outside the school system. To accommodate children in schools at the secondary level, there are some 84,000 institutions (1998–1999).

Post-secondary Education

India has one of the largest higher education systems in the world. It has universities, colleges, and Deemed Universities. State governments are responsible for establishment of state universities and colleges, and they provide planning grants for their development and non-planning grants for their maintenance. The Central Government is responsible for the major policies relating to higher education in the country. It provides grants to the UGC and establishes central universities. The Central Government is also responsible for the declaration of Educational Institutions as "Deemed to be University" on the recommendation of the UGC. The Constitution gives exclusive legislative power to the Central Government for coordination and determination of standards in institutions of higher education or research and scientific and technical institutions.

Presently there are sixteen central universities in the country. There are thirty-seven institutions, which have been declared "Deemed to be Universities" by the Central Government.

There are three principle levels of qualifications within the higher education system: bachelor/undergraduate level, master's/post-graduate level, and doctoral/pre-doctoral level.

Undergraduate work usually lasts between one and three years, while post-graduate work lasts about two years. Postgraduate work can be course-oriented without a thesis or research. Admission to post-graduate programs in engineering and technology is won on the basis of placement on Graduate Aptitude Tests.

Pre-doctoral programs can be entirely research-based or involve course work. Students are expected to write a substantial thesis based on original research.

Technical Education

Technical education offers great opportunities for adding value to products and services and thereby contributing to the national economy and improving the quality of life of the people. Technical education is being improved by modernization, by promoting institution–industry interaction, by providing continuing education to upgrade the skill and knowledge of technical personnel working in industry and service sectors, and by setting up the Technology Development Missions to meet the emerging challenges in science and technology.

Private Schools

While most students enroll in government schools, the number of private institutions is increasing at all educational levels. Indians have a right to establish institutions to provide education in their native language and with a religious or cultural emphasis, although the school must conform to state regulations of teaching standards.

Financing Education

India spends 3.8 percent of its GNP on education. From 1968 onward, the goal has been to devote 6 percent of national income on education. In spite of resource constraints as well as competing priorities, the budgetary expenditure on education by the Center and States as percentage of Gross National Product has steadily increased from 0.8 percent in 1951–1952, to 3.3 percent in 1994–1995.

Total budgetary expenditure on education by the Education Departments of the Center and States has increased. In terms of the share in total budgetary expenditure, education spending has increased from 7.9 percent in 1951–1952 to 11.1 percent in 1995–1996.

Adult Education

Until the end of World War I, there had been very little progress in the sphere of adult education. What there was was confined to night schools in cities. However, some of the Indian rulers of the princely States of Baraboda, Travancore, and Mysore had provided extended financial support to night schools. They also set up rural libraries. The national leaders who steered the freedom movement were also concerned with the question of educating the masses as a large part of the independence agenda. When the Congress Governments came to power in some provinces in 1937, adult literacy and education were included among the goals.

Literacy Rates

The strongest indication of the success of the Indian educational system is the tremendous rise in literacy rates. (See figure 3.6 and table 3.11.)

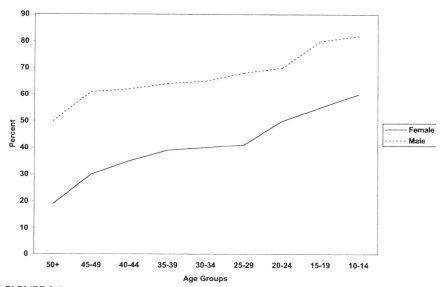

FIGURE 3.6
Literacy by Gender and Age Groups: 1995

TABLE 3.11
Literacy by Gender: 1901–1997

Year	Males	Females	Percent
1901	9.83	0.60	5.35
1911	10.56	1.05	5.92
1921	12.21	1.81	7.16
1931	15.59	2.93	9.50
1941	24.90	7.30	16.10
1951	29.95	7.93	16.67
1961	34.44	12.95	24.02
1971	39.45	18.69	29.45
1981	56.50	29.85	43.67
1991	64.13	39.29	52.21
1997	73.00	50.00	62.00

Eradication of illiteracy has been one of the major concerns of the Indian government since Independence. But the eradication of illiteracy from a nation that is the second most populated in the world is not an easy process. This was recognized in the 1980s when the National Literacy Mission was formed on May 5, 1988 to being a new sense of urgency to adult education. The literacy campaign was started in Kerala. During the last ten years, 556 districts out of 588 have been covered under the program and 259 are in the post-literacy phase, eighty-five are in the continuing education phase. The literacy rate in India has risen from 52 percent in 1991 to 62 percent in 1997. (See table A.1 in the appendix.) The wide gap between male and female literacy at last seems to be narrowing, as are the urban and rural differences.

The goals of the National Literacy Mission are to attain a literacy rate of 75 percent by 2005. The mission seeks to achieve this goal by bringing functional literacy to the nonliterate in the fifteen-to-thirty-five age group. The total literacy campaign offers individuals a second chance where they missed the opportunity for, or were denied access to, mainstream formal education.

School Enrollment Rates

The Indian Constitution calls for eight years of compulsory education for girls and boys ages six to fourteen. But enrollment rates vary tremendously. In some states, primary school enrollment for girls is 100 percent, in other areas it barely reaches 60 percent.

Half the girls who start primary school drop out before completion—most during the first year. Of those who go on to middle school, another 20 percent do not finish, and of the remaining girls who enter secondary school, 10 percent leave before graduation.

Despite high dropout rates, the school enrollment rates of girls have increased considerably over the past several decades. India now has 67 million children aged six to ten who are attending primary school, but 28 million to 32 million primary school-aged children who are not. (See figure 3.7.)

About 15 to 20 percent of children in India do not attend school regularly. About 40 percent of those enrolled drop out before completing the primary school cycle. Learning achievement is low. Despite progress in improving equity, gender and caste disparities persist in most education environments. And as could be expected in a nation of India's size and diversity, there are wide variations between and within states in the efficiency and equity of primary education.

There are about 888,000 educational institutions in the country with an enrollment of about 149.4 million children ages six through fourteen enrolled. This is about 82 percent of the children in this age group. (See figure 3.8.)

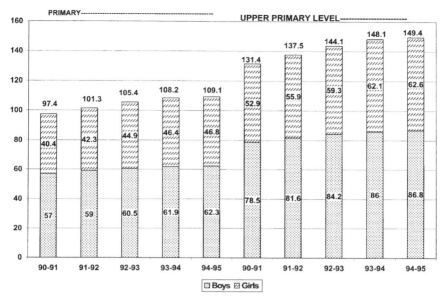

FIGURE 3.7
Enrollment up to Primary and Upper Primary Level (Figures in Millions)

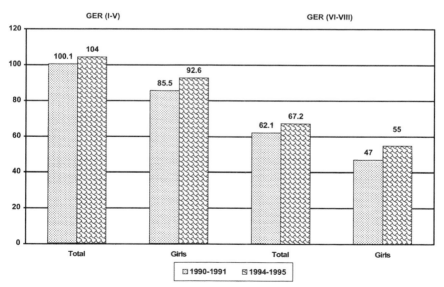

FIGURE 3.8
Gross Enrollment Ratio

In 1996, elementary and middle level schools enrolled about 110 million pupils, and secondary schools enrolled 69 million. Total yearly enrollment in institutions of higher education was 6.1 million. India has around 581,300 primary and upper primary schools, many of them one-room (or even open-air) operations with poorly paid teachers. There are also some 84,000 secondary schools, about 200 recognized universities, and 5,000 technical, arts, and science colleges. (See tables A.4, A.5, A.6, and A.7 in the appendix.)

Reforms in the Current Educational System

Proposed education reforms in India focus on increasing female enrollment, improving educational achievement, strengthening the community involvement, improving teaching and learning materials and providing in-service teacher training. Increasing the financing for primary education, improving the quality of the teachers and school infrastructures, and meeting health and safety codes are also included in the long-term reform program.

CHINA

Background Information

China, officially called the People's Republic of China, occupies much of Eastern Asia. It is the third largest country in area, after Russia and Canada. China borders Russia, Mongolia, and North Korea on the north; Pakistan, Afghanistan, Tajikistan, Kyrgyzstan, and Kazakhstan on the west; India, Nepal, Bhuta, Myanmar (Burma), Laos, and Vietnam on the South; and the Pacific Ocean and its extensions on the east. Over 1.3 billion people live in China and it is the most populous country on earth—more than one-fifth of the world's population. Three-fourths of the population live in rural villages. Even though a relatively low proportion of people live in cities, the actual number of city dwellers is larger than the total population of any country in that area except India.

The Communist Party controls China's government. Revolutionary forces took power in 1949. It is an authoritarian style government that imposes strict censorship and administers harsh penalties to nonconformists. The state monitors and regulates all phases of its citizens' activities. The Chinese Communist Party dominates policy making and policy execution through its members in the government. Within the governmental structure, the highest voice in the legislature is the National People's Congress (NCP). In practice, however, the most powerful unit is the cabinet, called the State Council, which is headed by the Premier.

China's burgeoning population has long been of major concern to the government, which in 1979 instituted a mandatory family policy of only one child per family. Although this policy has slowed down the birthrate and population increases, it has done so at the cost of females. It has created an uneven balance in the population between sexes. Because males are traditionally favored, many female fetuses are aborted and baby girls are often sent to orphanages, abandoned, allowed to die of neglect, or even killed by their parents.

More than 90 percent of China's inhabitants speak Chinese, the language of the Han people. There are many Chinese dialects. Most speak Mandarin Chinese. Putonghua, the standard form of Mandarin spoken in Beijing, is China's official spoken language. China's approximately 100 million minority people have their own spoken languages, which include Mongolian, Tibetan, Miao, Yi, Uygur, and Kazakh.

In 1949, the Communist party officially eliminated organized religion in China. Traditional religions of China were Confucianism, Taoism, and Buddhism. Islam and Christianity are the more formal and organized religions practiced in China today.

Basis of the Educational System—Principles and Legislation

Since 1978, the Chinese government has promulgated such codes as the Decree for The People's Republic of China, the Law of Compulsory Education of the People's Republic of China, the Law of Teachers of the People's Republic of China, the Law of Protection over Juveniles of the People's Republic of China, the Education Law of the People's Republic of China, the Law of Higher Education of the People's Republic of China, and has released more than ten secondary education administration regulations. The Ministry of Education has issued more than 200 sets of administrative rules and regulations facilitating the development of different forms of education.[1]

Since 1949, the Communists have instituted a vast and varied educational system that has repeatedly shifted the focus from ideological imperatives to practical efforts to train workers to compete in the modern world. During the Cultural Revolution, all schools were closed for some time as Mao tried to rid them of "liberal" intellectuals. The resulting decline in Chinese education was profound. Since the mid-1980s, there has been a growing desire for academic quality and an emphasis on expanding scientific knowledge and providing vocational and technical skills, especially for women. Most of these reforms, however, have not yet reached the millions of children living in remote villages.[2]

Control of the Educational System

China has an established education system with the government as its major investor. Currently, local government plays a major role in compulsory education and central and provincial governments are dominant in higher education. In occupational and adult education, industrial organizations play a major role. Businesses and public institutions are coming to the forefront as a crucial part of the education system.

The Ministry of Education of the PRC is the supreme education administration body in China, and is responsible for administering laws, regulations, guidelines and policies of the central government; planning the development of education; integrating and coordinating educational initiatives and programs nationwide; and maneuvering and guiding education reform nationwide.[3]

Organization of the Educational System

China's education system is composed of four components: basic education, which comprises preschool education; primary school (six years); secondary school (three years); and senior school (three years).

Pre-primary Education

Children from ages three to six usually attend kindergartens near their homes, where they learn basic skills. They are taught values and virtues such as truth, kindness, and beauty.

Compulsory Education

In 1986, nine years of education—six years of primary and three years of junior middle school—became compulsory for both girls and boys. (See table A.3 in the appendix.)

Primary School

In primary school, which has been extended to six years, students are required to take a variety of subjects such as Chinese language, fundamental mathematics, and moral education. They are also encouraged to become involved in sports and extracurricular activities. In recent years, foreign languages such as English became an optional course in the latter part of this six-year period.

Junior High School

In junior high school, students begin to study a variety of science subjects. They are also taught Chinese history and the history of foreign countries. Geography is also a required course at this level. Educators of all levels attach great importance to the teaching of English, the second official second language, in most of the high schools. At the same time, physical education is encouraged.

Senior High School

At the senior high school level, students are encouraged to take a greater interest in specific subject areas. To encourage students to achieve, teachers often create competitions. The "Olympic Series" are the most common competitions. But the most important thing for students in school is preparation for the national college entrance examination. The grade achieved on that examination largely determines what courses of study will be pursued by the student and where.

Post-secondary Education

The main task of higher education in China is to train individuals for all the sectors of the country's development. Universities, colleges, and institutes, which make up China's higher educational system, offer four- or five-year undergraduate programs as well as special two- or three-year programs. Students who have completed a first degree may apply to enter graduate schools.

Chinese higher education is now characterized by the *key-point system*. Under this system, the most promising students are placed in selected key-point schools, which specialize in training an academic elite. University education remains difficult to attain; as many as 2 million students compete each year through entrance examinations for 500,000 university openings. Students finishing secondary school may also attend junior colleges and a variety of technical and vocational schools. Among the most prominent comprehensive universities in China are Beijing University, Fudan University in Shanghai, Nanjing University, Nankai University in Tianjin, Wuhan University, Northwest University in Xi'an, and Zhongshan University in Guangzhou. Prestigious science and technical universities include Qinghua Technical and Engineering University in Beijing, Tongji University in Shanghai, and the Chinese University of Science and Technology in Hefei.

In the past, students received free university education but upon graduation were required to accept jobs in state-owned industries. In 1994, the government instituted a pilot program whereby the state allowed university students the option of paying their own tuition in exchange for the freedom to find their own jobs after graduation. This enabled graduates who paid their way to choose better paying jobs with foreign companies in China, or to demand better pay from state-owned enterprises. By the late 1990s, all incoming university students were required to pay their own tuition, although government loans were available.[4]

Certain fields of study have grown in popularity in Chinese higher education. While engineering and science remain very popular, other fields, including medicine, economics, literature, and law, have grown considerably in recent years. Another trend has been the rapid increase in the number of advanced students who study abroad, mainly in North America, Europe, and Japan. In 1978, at the beginning of the reform period, approximately 11,000 Chinese students went abroad to study. By 1996 more than 163,000 Chinese students were studying abroad.

Higher education includes junior college, bachelors, masters, and doctoral degree programs. Junior colleges usually last two to three years; bachelors programs four years (medical and some engineering and technical programs last five years); masters program two to three years; doctoral program three years.

Financing Education

Funds needed by schools directly controlled by the central government come from the central government. Schools controlled by local governments are supported by local finance; schools sponsored by townships and village governments and by public institutions are mainly financed by the sponsor institutions and subsidized by local government funds.

China's educational fund has been increased on a yearly basis since 1978. The educational input in 1998 reached RMB294.906 billion.

China provides free education at the university level, and those families who have financial difficulties received subsides. But in recent years, the number of paying students increased because of educational reform.

Medium-Level Occupational and Polytechnic Education

Since the 1980s, Chinese occupational and polytechnic education has experienced rapid developments. The schools are mainly middle-level professional, polytechnic schools and occupational middle schools as well as shorter occupational and technical training programs of various forms.

Adult Education

Adult education comprises schooling, anti-literacy education, and other programs oriented to adult groups. China's adult education has evolved rapidly since the end of World War II. Up to 1999, there were 871 colleges and universities that focused on adult education and some 800 correspondence-based and evening adult education programs launched by colleges, offering 1,157,700 seats to those pursuing junior college and bachelors programs, and granted diplomas to 88,200 people.

Alternative Forms of Education

Higher education examination programs for the self-taught has been increasingly popular. In 1998, there were 224 disciplines launched under this program. Up to the first half of 2000, accumulated registration for such examinations reached 104.04 million. More than 2.9 million people earned their junior colleges and bachelor degrees, and 401,500 people passed the secondary technical eligibility examinations under this program.

Literacy Rates

In the last four decades, the literacy rate has increased from less than 10 percent to 68 percent. But in 1990, of the 22 percent of the country's population who were illiterate, 70 percent were women.

In 1998, some 134,200 anti-illiteracy classes were launched nationwide to bring benefits to 3,208,900 illiterate persons. (See table A.1 in the appendix.)

School Enrollment Rates

Fewer girls than boys enter school and more drop out, especially in rural areas, where they are often kept out of school to help with farming and household chores. Another obstacle for many families is the tuition charged by the schools, and although some private and public assistance is available, many rural girls have no access to these funds. In addition, the typical farm family sees no advantage in educating a daughter who will soon be getting married and moving into her in-laws' house.

In the 1996–1997 academic year, China had almost 140,000 million pupils enrolled in primary schools, and 72 million students enrolled in secondary schools. By contrast, enrollments in 1949 had been about 24 million in primary schools and 1.25 million in secondary schools. There were almost 6.1 million students enrolled in institutions of higher learning in 1996. (See tables A.4, A.5, A.6, and A.7 in the appendix.)

As of 1999, there were 582,300 primary schools countrywide with an enrollment of 135,549 million. The enrollment rate of schoolchildren reached 99.09 percent with a five-year retention rate of 92.48 percent. Moderate development was also witnessed in junior middle schools countrywide.

By 1999, there were 64,400 common junior middle schools nationwide with 58,115 million students enrolled. There were 14,100 common high schools nationwide with enrollment of 10,497 million students. As of 1998, there were 10,074 occupational middle schools nationwide, with 5,416 million students enrolled.

Since the 1980s, Chinese occupational and polytechnic education has experienced rapid development. Up to 1997, there were 33,464 occupational and polytechnic schools nationwide with an enrollment of 18, 697 million; more than 2,100 employment training schools provided training for about 1 million people.

As of 1999, there were 3,962 secondary technical schools nationwide with an enrollment of 5,155,000. Enrollments in finance and economics, sports and arts programs went up steadily, while disciplines in the technical subjects went down gradually. In 1999, there were 8,317 vocational senior schools nationwide with 4,438,400 students enrolled and 4,098 polytechnic schools with 1,500,000 students enrolled.

As of 1999, there were 1,071 common colleges and universities countrywide offering 2,754,500 seats to those applying for junior college and bachelor programs, 19,900 seats to those applying for doctoral programs, and 72,300 to masters programs applicants.

In 1998, there were 421 seats in adult education schools targeted for farmers. Technical schools with an enrollment of 200,200, and middle schools with an enrollment of 439,200 provided training for more than 80 million people, or 12.2 percent of the rural labor force. (See table 3.12.)

TABLE 3.12
Number of Student Enrollment by Level and Type of School

Unit: 10,000 persons

Year	Regular Institutions of Higher Education	Secondary Schools	Specialized Secondary Schools	Technical Schools	Teacher Training Schools	Regular Secondary	Senior	Junior	Vocational Schools	Primary Schools	Kindergartens
1952	19.1	314.5	63.6	29.0	34.5	249.0	26.0	223.0		5110.0	42.4
1957	44.1	708.1	77.8	48.2	29.6	628.1	90.4	537.7		6428.3	108.8
1962	83.0	833.5	53.5	35.3	18.2	752.8	133.9	618.9	26.7	6923.9	144.6
1965	67.4	1431.8	54.7	39.2	15.5	933.8	130.8	803.0	443.3	11620.9	171.3
1970	4.8	2648.3	6.4	3.2	3.2	2641.9	349.7	2292.2		10528.0	
1975	50.1	4536.8	70.7	40.5	30.2	4466.1	1163.7	3302.4		15094.1	620.0
1978	85.6	6637.2	88.9	52.9	36.0	6548.3	1553.1	4995.2		14624.0	787.7
1980	114.4	5677.8	124.3	76.1	48.2	5508.1	969.8	4538.3	45.4	14627.0	1150.8
1985	170.3	5092.6	157.1	100.9	56.2	4706.0	741.1	3964.8	229.5	13370.2	1479.7
1986	188.0	5321.6	175.7	114.6	61.1	4889.9	773.4	4116.6	256.0	13182.5	1629.0
1987	195.9	5403.1	187.4	122.3	65.1	4948.1	773.7	4174.4	267.6	12835.9	1807.8
1988	206.6	5246.1	205.2	136.8	68.3	4761.5	746.0	4015.5	279.4	12535.8	1854.5
1989	208.2	5054.0	217.7	149.3	68.5	4554.0	716.1	3837.9	282.3	12373.1	1847.7
1990	206.3	5105.4	224.4	156.7	67.7	4586.0	717.3	3868.7	295.0	12241.4	1972.2
1991	204.4	5226.8	227.7	161.6	66.1	4683.5	722.9	3960.6	315.6	12164.2	2209.3
1992	218.4	5354.4	240.8	174.3	66.6	4770.8	704.9	4065.9	342.8	12201.3	2428.2
1993	253.6	5383.7	282.0	209.8	72.2	4739.1	656.9	4082.2	362.6	12421.2	2552.5
1994	279.9	5707.1	319.8	241.4	78.4	4981.7	664.9	4316.7	405.6	12822.6	2630.3
1995	290.6	6191.5	372.2	287.4	84.8	5371.0	713.2	4657.8	448.3	13195.2	2711.2
1996	302.1	6635.7	422.8	334.8	88.0	5739.7	769.3	4970.4	473.3	13615.0	2666.3
1997	317.4	6995.2	465.4	374.3	91.1	6017.9	850.1	5167.8	511.9	13995.4	2519.0

Reforms in the Current Educational System

As a whole, education in China, the world's most populous country with extremely unbalanced economic and cultural development, lags far behind other industrialized nations. The proportions of graduates from primary, junior and senior middle schools who enter schools of higher levels is an important indicator reflecting the educational level of a nation. According to a demographic survey conducted in 1995, 1 percent, approximately 100,000 people, did so.

The Chinese government regards education as a strategic priority, and promotes China's Agenda for Educational Reform and Development. By the end of the twentieth century, proposed goals included K–9 compulsory education nationwide, eliminating illiteracy among the middle aged population, actively supporting 100 universities in key subjects, and providing adequate support for occupational polytechnic education and adult education.[5]

Notes

1. See <www.cernet.edu.cn/english/eduction/index.php>.
2. Naomi Neft and Ann D. Levine, *Where Women Stand: An International Report on the Status of Women in 140 Countries, 1997–1998.* (New York: Random House, 1997).
3. Ibid.
4. Ibid.
5. Ibid.

JAPAN

Background Information

Japan is an archipelago in East Asia, located in the North Pacific Ocean off the coast of Asia. Japan is comprised of four main islands, Honshu, Hokkareto, Kynshus, and Shikskuo, in addition to more than 30,000 smaller ones. The Japanese call their country Nikon or Nippon, which means "origin of the sun." It is derived from the country's geographical position—east of the Chinese Empire that historically dominated them.

Despite its small size and few natural resources, Japan is a highly industrialized nation and a major world economic power.

Most of the population lives on plains and lowlands found along the country's major rivers, on the lowest slopes of mountain ranges, and along the seacoast. This concentration of people makes Japan one of the world's most crowded countries. Densities are especially high in the urban areas between Tokyo and Kobe, where 45 percent of the country's population is packed into only 17 percent of its land area. About 77 percent live in urban centers.

Japan covers a total area of 377,837 square kilometers. Together, the four main islands make up 95 percent of Japan's territory.

Japan is a parliamentary democracy. An emperor acts as the formal head of state, although his official status under the Constitution is the "symbol" of the Japanese nation and its people. Japan is a unitary state, in which the authority of the central government is superior to that of the country's prefectuaral governments. But Japan's forty-seven prefectures and several thousand cities, town, and village governments enjoy a significant degree of autonomy over local affairs.

Japanese, the official language of Japan, has a number of regional dialects that at times are incomprehensible to speakers of other dialects. Ainu is Japan's only other indigenous language. It is now nearly extinct. Korean and Chinese residents of Japan usually speak Japanese as their first language. Many Japanese study foreign languages, most commonly English.

Japan is primarily a secular society in which religion is not a central factor in most people's daily lives. Yet certain religious practices help define the society. Most Japanese people profess at least some religious affiliation. The dominant religions are Buddhism and Shintoism, a religion that originated in Japan. There is a small Christian minority (1 percent). Today, about two-thirds of Japan's Christians are Protestants, and about one-third are Roman Catholics. Small communities of other faiths are present in Japan as well.

Basis of the Educational System—Principles and Legislation

Based on the concept of equal educational opportunities for all, the Japanese Education Ministry has set standards for educational curricula in order to ensure a nationwide standard of education from kindergarten to upper secondary school. An ordinance based on School Education Law stipulates the educational content of kindergartens and the number of kindergarten weeks per year, as well as setting subjects in elementary schools, lower and upper secondary schools, and schools for the blind, the deaf, and the disabled.[1]

The Japan Study by the U.S. Department of Education indicates one possible explanation for Japan's success in math and science, which is representative of all of its success in education—the Japanese educational system actively builds students' motivation to learn. Each section of the Japanese education system offers vivid examples of how the system works to motivate Japanese students. (See table 3.13.)

The Japanese Education Ministry emphasizes creating well-rounded students at the elementary and junior high school levels through the various subject areas in the national curriculum. They set standard hours per subject in the national elementary school curriculum, emphasizing subjects such as music, arts, and handicrafts, homemaking, physical education,

TABLE 3.13
Standard Number of Hours Spent in Various Subjects

Subject	Grade					
	1	*2*	*3*	*4*	*5*	*6*
Arithmetic and Science	136	175	280	280	280	280
Life Activities	102	105	105	105	105	105
Japanese language	306	315	280	280	210	210
Music, arts & handicrafts and homemaking; Physical education; Moral education; Special Activities	306	315	315	350	420	420

Source: Jichi Sogo Center, 1991
Note: Implemented in April 1992

and moral education, as well as math and sciences. The standards also devote a large amount of time to Japanese language and life activities, a subject that gives younger students personal life experiences in preparation for classroom-oriented science. In the life activity classes, students participate in picking flowers, catching frogs and insects, raising rabbits, and watching falling stars.[2]

Japanese schools focus on all subjects to produce a well-rounded education that serves several purposes: student engagement, strong classroom relationships, and student motivation. Japanese eighth graders on average spend between thirty minutes and one hour doing math and science homework each day. Japanese's students participate in after-school activities that may foster higher academic performance.[3]

Control of the Educational System

The educational administration is organized into a three-tiered structure with national, perfectural, and municipal components—all under the general supervision of the Ministry of Education. The Ministry has a considerable measure of authority over curricular standards, textbooks, and school financing. Through its central and advisory role, the Ministry of Education has made the educational system of Japan among the best in the world.

Organization of the Educational System

The educational system is organized into a 6–3–3–4 system of formal education aimed at realizing the principle of equal opportunity for education: elementary schools (*shogakko*), lower secondary schools (*chugakko*), or upper secondary schools (*kotogakko*), and *daigaku*, or universities. In addition, there are kindergartens for preschool education and various types of vocational and technical schools and universities which meet practical lifestyle needs.

Pre-primary Education

Schooling generally begins in preschool (*yochien*). The objective of preschool is to teach fundamental skills to children from age three until they are old enough to start primary school. Pre-primary education fosters physical and mental development.

Compulsory Education

Nine years of education is compulsory for both boys and girls. All children between the ages of six and fifteen are required to study at elementary and lower secondary schools. (See table A.3 in the appendix.)

Elementary Education

Schools in Japan provide general education for children aged six to twelve. Children between six and twelve attend elementary school, where they are taught six years of general elementary education corresponding to their physical and mental development.

Lower Secondary School

Lower secondary education follows the general curriculum. It aims to provide children from ages twelve to fifteen with three years of general secondary education. The curriculum of the lower secondary schooling became a rallying point for women's groups following World War II, when they succeeded in tearing down age-old gender stereotypes by making home economics classes compulsory for both boys and girls. In the 1950s, with the return of traditional attitudes, the curriculum was revised and boys were required to take industrial arts while girls took only home economics. Again, women's groups mobilized and in 1993, home economics became compulsory for both boys and girls. The following year, home economics became mandatory for all students in upper secondary schools.

There are student examinations for granting Equivalency Certificates for lower secondary school graduates who are exempted from or who have postponed compulsory attendance. This examination is aimed at students who have been unable to attend a lower secondary school due to illness or other unavoidable circumstances; and for students who have graduated from schools for foreign nationals. The examination determines whether students are equivalent to or above the level of lower secondary school graduates in terms of academic achievement. Those who pass are granted the qualifications necessary to enter upper secondary school.[4]

Upper Secondary Education

Upper secondary school provides children who have completed compulsory education with a general and specialized upper secondary education. The courses in upper secondary school include general educational courses and specialized subject courses: agriculture, industry, business, fisheries, home economics, nursing, science and mathematics, English language and others. As of 1994 an integrated course program was designed to provide general and specialized education mainly in an integrated manner or on an elective basis by the students.[5]

Unified Lower and Upper Secondary Education

Unified upper and secondary education became a part of the educational system in April 1999. By enabling students and parents/guardians to select a six-year course consistent with the present lower and upper secondary system, the unified lower secondary course promotes further diversification of secondary education and further stresses the importance of individuality. In the unified lower and upper secondary education system, there are three school types: secondary schools, in which lower and secondary education are integrated into one school; joint school type, in which lower and upper secondary schools are located on the same site; and cooperative type, in which existing municipal lower secondary and prefecture upper secondary schools cooperate in organizing the curriculum, and student teaching exchange.

The Ministry of Education is promoting the furnishing of at least one such school per upper secondary school district (there are about 500 upper secondary school districts in Japan) so that students can choose the lower and upper secondary education they wish.[6]

Post-secondary Education

Most high schools and universities admit students based on scores received on entrance exams. Japan's high schools and universities are highly competitive mainly because the most prestigious jobs typically go to graduates of elite universities. Important and prestigious universities include the University of Tokyo, Kyoto University, and Keio University in Tokyo.

Higher education institutions in Japan consist of universities, junior colleges, colleges of technology, and specialized training colleges that offer advanced courses.

Private Schools

Since the end of World War II, the number of private educational institutions has increased. About 1 percent of elementary schools and 5 percent of junior high schools are private. Nearly 25 percent of high schools are private. Whether public or private, high schools are ranked informally according to their success at placing graduates into prestigious universities.

Financing Education

Japan ranks among the top nations in the world in educational attainment. Education is free and compulsory for elementary and junior high schools (grades one through nine). The government invests a great deal of money into education to ensure quality and accessibility.

Alternative Forms of Education

Other kinds of educational opportunities available in Japan include vocational and technology colleges and the popular University of the Air, which focuses on radio, television, and other media. Enrollment began at the University of the Air in 1989 and by 1993 the student body numbered 48,000, half of whom were women.

In addition to academic courses of study, some students, particularly at the junior high school level, enroll in specialized private schools called *juku*. Often translated into English as "cram schools," these schools offer supplementary lessons after school hours and on weekends, and tutoring is available to improve scores on senior high school entrance examinations. Students who are preparing for college entrance exams attend special schools called *yobiko*. A disappointing score on a college entrance examination means that a student must settle for a lesser college, decide not to attend college at all, or study for a year or more at *yobiko* in preparation to retaking the examination. Some adolescents choose to spend after school time at *juku*, privately owned academies that provide supplementary classes for students who pay a fee. *Juku* offers challenging and remedial courses for those who feel public education does not offer enough.[7]

Literacy Rates

Japan's adult literacy is among the highest in the world, at 99 percent for both men and women.

School Enrollment Rates

More than 99 percent of elementary school aged students attend school. Most students who finish junior high school continue and advance to senior high schools (grades ten through twelve). Approximately one-third of senior high school graduates enroll in higher education.

Women constitute 40 percent of higher education students—only 29 percent in the universities, but 92 percent in the junior colleges. In postgraduate studies, Japanese women make up 19 percent of master's degree and 17 percent of doctoral degree candidates. (See tables A.4, A.5, A.6, and A.7 in the appendix.)

Reforms in the Current Educational Systems

Proposed reforms of the Japanese educational system consist mainly of eliminating the remaining uniformity and rigidity of education at all levels. The country also strives for the advancement of "individuality" through education by improving moral education, encouraging greater freedom, improving teacher training, and diversifying higher education. Reforms seek to encourage student's self-expression and increase flexibility in curricula and classroom procedures.

Notes

1. See <www. monbu.go.jp>.
2. See <http://www.ed.gov/pubs/ResearchToday/98-3038.html>.

3. Ibid.
4. See <www.monbu.go.jp>.
5. Ibid.
6. Ibid.
7. Ibid.

Country Profiles: Oceania

NEW ZEALAND

Background Information

New Zealand is a self-governing country in the South Pacific Ocean situated southeast of Australia. It is a member of the Commonwealth of Nations. It comprises two large islands—North and South Island—and numerous smaller islands including Stewart Island to the south of South Island. New Zealand comprises a land area of 270,534 square kilometers.

As of 1991, the population of New Zealand is 3,434,950. The 2000 estimate is 3,697,850, giving the country an overall population density of fourteen persons per square kilometer. Nearly three-fourths of the population reside on the North Island. Eighty-six percent of the people live in urban areas, and about half of these are in the four largest cities.

New Zealand is divided into twelve local government regions and four unitary authorities. Executive action is taken on behalf of the governor-general, who is appointed by the British monarch. The governor general, prime minister, and the ministers heading the various governmental departments form the legislative body of the government. The primary administrative body of New Zealand is the cabinet, which consists of the prime minister and the ministers in charge of departments.

English and Maori are the official languages in New Zealand, although the country is predominately English-speaking. Almost all of the Maori speak English, and only about 50,000 (15 percent) are considered fluent Maori speakers. Other Polynesian and European languages are spoken by a small percentage of the population.

A large majority of the New Zealand population is Christian. The primary denominations are Anglican (22 percent), Presbyterian (16 percent), and Roman Catholic (15 percent). Methodist, Baptist, and other Protestant denominations are also represented. Most of the Maori are members of the Ratana and Rignatu Christian sect. Jews, Hindus, and Buddhists constitute small minorities. About 21 percent profess no religious faith.

Control of the Educational System

The Ministry of Education dictates many of the educational policies and regulations, thus controlling the educational system of New Zealand.

Pre-primary Education

Pre-primary education is not compulsory in New Zealand but many families are aware of the benefits of having their children attend pre-primary schooling. In some areas, subsidized kindergartens are provided for children between three and five years of age. In pre-primary education, children are taught the skills and habits that will enhance their ability to learn and adapt to the next level of schooling.

Compulsory Education

Education is free and compulsory for children between the ages of six and sixteen, but children may enter schools at age five and continue until they are nineteen. (See table A.3 in the appendix.)

Primary education consists of infant classes during the first two years, and six annual grades, designated as standards 1, 2, 3, and 4 and forms I and II. Free secondary education is available to all children who have completed form II or who are age fourteen. On the completion of the third year of secondary education, pupils take a national examination for a school certificate, which attests to their completion of basic secondary education. The prerequisite for admission to university study is either attaining a sixth form certificate or passing the university entrance examination.[1]

Post-secondary Education

The university system in New Zealand comprises seven separate government-funded universities. At the university level, students are able to receive a variety of degrees—undergraduate, graduate, and doctoral. Students usually spend four to eight years in higher education.

Private School

New Zealand has numerous types of non-public schools, such as special institutions for handicapped individuals, private schools, and religious affiliated schools. There are private schools at all levels of the educational system. Such schools require tuition fees

Financing Education

Compulsory public education is free of charge. Schools not funded by the government require tuition payments. For higher education many students receive help from the government or take out loans.

Adult Education

There is an extensive adult-education program throughout the country that is maintained by the National Council of Adult Education. About 88,430 students attend polytechnic institutions.

Alternative Forms of Education

New Zealand continues to experiment with innovative school attendance schedules aimed at enhancing students' academic progress, improving family life, and reducing stress for both students and teachers. In New Zealand, 230 local boards of education chose to change from the established three-term school year to a four-term school year that has proved successful when tried in six schools in 1993. The experimental

schools reported that under shorter ten-week terms, pupil teacher interaction improved, students settled down to their studies more quickly
after term breaks, and they stayed more motivated throughout the term.
Officials estimated that the new plan would be instituted nationally by
1996.[2]

Literacy Rates

Literacy rates in New Zealand are among the highest in the world for
both men and women at 99 percent. (See table A.1 in the appendix.)

School Enrollment Rates

In 1997, there were 2,296 public and private primary schools in New
Zealand. These schools had an enrollment of 357,600 students. Some students attended composite schools, which combine primary and secondary
education and include a correspondence school. Students attending secondary and special schools numbered 433,300. (See tables A.4, A.5, A.6,
and A.7 in the appendix.)

Reforms in the Current Educational System

New Zealand has a variety of reforms on the table. One of the major
proposed reforms is to increase the quality and access of education to all
school-aged children. Another primary concern is to further advance its
adult education programs.

Notes

1. "New Zealand," *Microsoft Encarta Encyclopedia Standard 2001*, CD–ROM.
(Redmond, Wash.: Microsoft Corporation, 2001).
2. Ibid.

AUSTRALIA

Background Information

Australia is located in the Southern Hemisphere between the Indian and Pacific Oceans. It is a federation of six states—New South Wales, Queensland, South Australia, Tasmania, Victoria, and Western Australia—and two territories: Northern Territory and Australian Capital Territory (ACT), the site of the nation's capital. It extends for about 4,000 kilometers from east to west and for about 3,700 kilometers from north to south. Its coastline measures some 25,760 kilometers. Australia is 7,682,300 square kilometers, making it the smallest continent in the world, but the sixth largest country.

Australia is one of the most urbanized countries in the world. Its population is estimated at just over 19 million. Approximately 85 percent live in urban centers, with about a third residing in the two largest cities, Sydney and Melbourne. The most rapidly growing areas are the coastal regions near and between the mainland capitals in the east, southeast, and southwest. Four out of five Australians live on the closely-settled coastal plains that make up only about three percent of the country's land area.

Australia is a federal parliamentary democracy and a member of the Commonwealth of Nations. The Constitution of Australia, which became effective in 1901, is based on British parliamentary traditions, and includes elements of the United States system. The head of state is the British sovereign, and the head of the government is the Australian prime minister, who is responsible to the Australian Parliament. All powers not delegated to the federal government are reserved to the states.

The official language of Australia is English.

Australia has no single established church, and its Constitution guarantees freedom of worship. The population is predominately Christian. The largest single denominations are Roman Catholic (26 percent of the population) and the Anglican Church Australia (26 percent). Jewish, Buddhist, and Muslim worshippers make up a small portion of the population. The number of Buddhists and Muslims is increasing, reflecting the changing immigration patterns since the 1960s. A significant share of Australia's population claim to be nonreligious.

Control of the Educational System

Education is a state, rather than a federal, responsibility. In each state administration, the training and recruitment of teachers are centralized under a state education department. Authority is also concentrated in a State Department of Education. The political head is the minister of education, and the permanent official in charge is the director general of education. The main divisions of the department are those for primary, secondary, and technical education. Each is directed by a senior official; additional divisions, such as special education or in-service training, are specific to the states.

Through the 1980s, major changes in administrative organization took place in all systems in Australia. The idea was to transfer some of the authority to local regions and schools. A corporate style of management has become preferable, using criteria of rationalization, effectiveness, and economic efficiency to guide organizational decisions. Although states agree on many overall goals, disagreements among state authorities, powerful teachers' unions, and public groups promise the continuation of a politically volatile and changing administrative scene.

The governments of the states and territories manage all aspects of education except for the university sector.

Organization of the Educational System

The organizational system of education is very similar to that of Britain and the United States. School is not compulsory before the age of six. But pre-primary education is available throughout country. Formal schooling begins with primary education. School is compulsory from ages six to fifteen (sixteen in Tasmania), after which two more years of secondary schooling is optional. The tertiary level of education consists of vocational and technical schools, along with colleges and universities, and specialization schools.

Pre-primary Education

Education is provided in kindergartens and play centers for children from two to six years of age. The Australian Broadcasting Corporation conducts broadcasts for kindergarten children unable to attend such centers. Special provisions are made for children in isolated areas. These include Schools of Air—where children use two-way radios, television sets, video and cassette recorders, and computers to participate in classroom instruction—and correspondence schools.

Compulsory Education

Education is compulsory between the ages of six and fifteen in all states except Tasmania where the upper age limit is sixteen. Most children start their schooling at the age of five. (See table A.3 in the appendix.) State schools provide free secular education. Students may attend religious classes offered by the clergy of various denominations.

Primary schools are usually six years in duration to about the age of twelve. Within primary schools, students are grouped in grade levels and advance by annual promotion.

Most children transfer from the primary to the secondary school level at the age of twelve. Secondary education is offered for five or six years, generally in comprehensive schools. The minimum age for leaving school is fifteen (sixteen in Tasmania). Secondary schools, known as high schools and junior technical schools, provide five- or six-year courses that enable students to prepare for state examinations for university entrance. The commonwealth government conducts the educational program for all children in the territories. Secondary school curricula tend to focus on compulsory courses of traditional subjects coupled with a generous list of electives. Specialist services include educational, psychological, and vocational counseling, assistance for Aboriginal children and adults, programs offered in English as a second language, and courses for gifted and handicapped children. Foreign languages have not been well represented, despite continuous rhetoric about multiculturalism, and several ethnic groups have felt obliged to organize their own programs.[1]

Post-secondary Education, Higher Education, and Specialized Schools

Tertiary education is provided in self-governing universities and colleges of higher education and in institutes operating as part of the state-controlled Technical and Further Education (TAFE) systems.

In 1988, the federal government launched an assertive restructuring program to produce fewer, larger institutions, with each institution offering a broader educational profile. The process was to be assisted by the re-imposition of student fees and by amendments to central funding mechanisms. It was expected that the process would produce between thirty and thirty-five higher (and broader) educational institutions.

The original state-sponsored system guaranteed an even spread of universities, and it is still unusual for undergraduates to attend universities outside of their home states.

The commonwealth government maintains training colleges for the defense services, the Australian Forestry School in Canberra, and the School for Pacific Administration in Sydney, which conducts training programs that are attended primarily by civil service administrators from Papua New Guinea. The government also maintains the Australian Film, Television and Radio School, the Australian Maritime College and the National Institute of Dramatic Art. There are also technical and Further Education (TAFE) colleges that offer vocational and technical training.

In the early 1990s, there were thirty-seven universities including two private universities, and a large number of colleges offering advanced education in specific subject areas. Their combined annual enrollment in 1997 was 1,401,648. As with most other developed countries, women make up more than half of all higher education students.

Private and Public Schools

About three-fourths of Australian schools are public and 72 percent of students attend state schools. In addition to the state school system there are private schools, which are usually denominational and charge tuition fees. Since 1965, significant government funding has been provided to private schools. There has been a resurgence of interest in and a consequent increase of influence from this sector in recent years.

Financing Education

Almost three-fourths of Australians attend free government schools. The federal government is responsible for the total funding of higher education and provides supplementary funding to the states. In the late 1980s, a federal Australian Labor Party government intensified Commonwealth involvement at every level. For example, in addition to its long-standing financial role, it attempted to develop a stronger national or centralist perspective. Fees are generally higher at non-government schools.[2]

Literacy Rates

At 99 percent, literacy rates in Australia are among the highest in the world for both men and women. (See table A.1 in the appendix.)

School Enrollment Rates

Most children begin school at the age of five. More than two-thirds of the secondary school students remain until the end of year eleven, and more than half remain until the end of year twelve. In 1995, Australia had nearly 10,000 primary and secondary schools, with an annual enrollment of 1.9 million primary students and 2.4 million secondary students.

Women make up more than half of all higher education students. (See tables A.4, A.5, A.6, and A.7 in the appendix.)

Reforms in the Current Educational System

Proposed education reforms in Australia include attempts to increase the number of students in continuing education and to improve or expand programs to serve the whole population. Such measures have raised interest in system unification, including such issues as establishing common curricula and stronger Australian content, improving the transition from school to work, and providing equal opportunities for the Aboriginal, the disabled, and other groups designated as disadvantaged. The government has recently highlighted the contribution of Aboriginal cultures as well as of Australian studies. Other reforms proposed include improving teaching practices, curricula, school organization, teacher education and methods of assessment.

Australia has also tried to increase vocational offerings over the past decade. Educational planners sought to emulate Germany, which, compared with the size of its workforce, had four times as many apprentices as Australia and twice as many workers with non-university post-secondary training.[3]

Notes

1. "Australia," *Microsoft Encarta Encyclopedia Standard 2001*, CD–ROM. (Redmond, Wash.: Microsoft Corporation, 2001.
    2. Ibid.
    3. Ibid.

4

Public Perceptions Worldwide

As human beings we all seem to share some universal basic values, no matter where we live, whether it is in a small remote farm village in India, a rainforest in Brazil, the metropolitan city of London, or across the world in Beijing, China. In the year 2000–2001, Gallup International conducted the world's largest ever opinion poll in sixty countries around the globe. A representative sample of 50,000 people was asked: "What matters most in life?" The choices were as follows:

- To have a job.
- To get an education.
- To be faithful to my religion.
- To have a good standard of living.
- To live in a country where there is not war.
- To have a happy family life.
- To live in freedom.
- To live in a country without violence and corruption.
- To have good health.

The most common responses from around the world were to have good health and to have a happy family life.

Education came in second to last, as mattering most in life, only above the response, "Don't know." (See figure 4.1.)

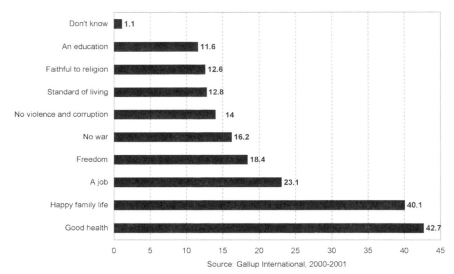

FIGURE 4.1
What Matters Most in Life?

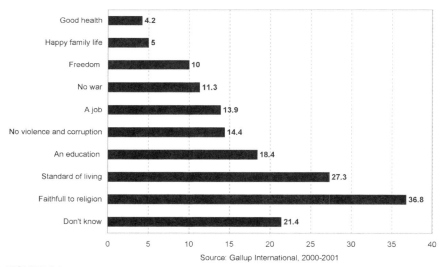

FIGURE 4.2
What Matters Least in Life?

In the survey the question was also reversed. The list of values remained the same but the question was now: "Which are the two things that you would say matter least in life?" This time, education came in fourth on the list of what matters least in life. Ranking above it were the responses, "Don't know," "Faithful to religion," and "Standard of living." (See figure 4.2.)

5

Conclusion

Global Perspectives on Social Issues: Education compares educational systems throughout the world and provides an international context by which to compare them. These components are set within each country's social, economic, and political contexts. It is important to look at the trends of these countries within those contexts, thereby allowing the reader to better understand the educational path of each nation.

Nations throughout the world vary in the kind of education and amount of schooling they provide and require. Some nations, including most European and North American countries, have well-developed economies and long-lasting educational systems. Almost all children in these countries receive an elementary education and most receive a secondary education. They also offer general education and vocational classes. In contrast many countries in Asia and less-developed countries have economic problems and can barely sustain enough schools for children to attend. In some areas of the world, children are placed in a classroom with four other grade levels and no toilets. In these areas, children rarely finish elementary education.

Enrollment and literacy rates are a good measure of education in various countries. The higher the enrollment and literacy rates, the higher the level of education within a country. It is also a good indicator of the status of women in a given country. Rates vary not only among countries, but also regions. Often the presence of centuries-old traditions, eco-nomic situations, and political climate will affect these statistics.

Cultural and political ideologies also shape the structure of education policies. These ideologies determine how education is administered and controlled. Most national governments have some control of public schooling. Government expenditures and funding vary from nation to nation. Some nations provide full funding while others spend only a small portion of their budget on education.

Internationally, education has been recognized as a basic human right. Consequently, all nations of the world are making concerted efforts to eradicate illiteracy and increase enrollment rates. Countries seek to make quality education a norm and accessible to all citizens. Most countries recognize that education is essential to a strong and prosperous nation, in part because education empowers individuals to be involved in public issues and allows them to debate them effectively in society. Throughout the world education also opens the door to higher paying jobs, a better standard of living, and a healthier, more productive life.

Moving into the twenty-first century, nations recognize that their suc-cess is measured by their ability to educate their citizens. It is now more commonly seen as a basic human right. It is through education that ig-norance and poverty will be eradicated. Education is a vital force for so-cial change. It is the foundation for a free and prosperous society, as well as a right of all children and an obligation of all governments.

Bibliography

"Argentina." *Microsoft Encarta Encyclopedia Standard 2001*, CD–ROM. Redmond, Wash.: Microsoft Corporation, 2001.

"Australia." *Microsoft Encarta Encyclopedia Standard 2001*, CD–ROM. Redmond, Wash.: Microsoft Corporation, 2001.

"Brazil." *Microsoft Encarta Encyclopedia Standard 2001*, CD–ROM. Redmond, Wash.: Microsoft Corporation, 2001.

"Canada." *Microsoft Encarta Encyclopedia Standard 2001*, CD–ROM. Redmond, Wash.: Microsoft Corporation, 2001.

Canadian Education Statistics Council. *Education Indicators in Canada: Report of the Pan–Canadian Education Indicators Program 1999*. Canadian Education Statistic Council. Toronto: February 2000.

"China." *Microsoft Encarta Encyclopedia Standard 2001*, CD–ROM. Redmond, Wash.: Microsoft Corporation, 2001.

"England." *Microsoft Encarta Encyclopedia Standard 2001*, CD–ROM. Redmond, Wash.: Microsoft Corporation, 2001.

Eurydice Unit. *Structures of Education, Initial Training and Adult Education Systems in Europe, Germany 1999*. Eurydice European Unit: Brussels, March 2000.

Eurydice Unit. *Structures of Education, Initial Training and Adult Education Systems in Europe, Italy 1999*. Eurydice European Unit: Brussels, March 2000.

Eurydice Unit. *Structures of Education, Initial Training and Adult Education Systems in Europe, Poland 1999*. Eurydice European Unit: Brussels, March 2000.

Eurydice Unit. *Structures of Education, Initial Training and Adult Education Systems in Europe, Spain 1999*. Eurydice European Unit: Brussels, March 2000.

Eurydice Unit. *Structures of Education, Initial Training and Adult Education Systems in Europe, United Kingdom 1999.* Eurydice European Unit: Brussels, March 2000.

"Egypt." *Microsoft Encarta Encyclopedia Standard 2001,* CD–ROM. Redmond, Wash.: Microsoft Corporation, 2001.

Francis, Paul A. *Hard Lessons: Primary Schools, Community, and Social Capital in Nigeria.* Washington, D.C.: World Bank, 1998.

"Germany." *Microsoft Encarta Encyclopedia Standard 2001,* CD–ROM. Redmond, Wash.: Microsoft Corporation, 2001.

Glenn, Charles L. *Educational Freedom in Eastern Europe.* Washington, D.C.: Cato Institute, 1997.

Haiducek, Nicholas J. *Japanese Education: Made in the U.S.A.* New York: Praeger, 1991.

"India." *Microsoft Encarta Encyclopedia Standard 2001,* CD–ROM. Redmond, Wash.: Microsoft Corporation, 2001.

Iram, Yaacov and Mirjam Schmida. *The Educational System of Israel.* Westport, Conn.: Greenwood Press, 1998.

"Iraq." *Microsoft Encarta Encyclopedia Standard 2001,* CD–ROM. Redmond, Wash.: Microsoft Corporation, 2001.

"Israel." *Microsoft Encarta Encyclopedia Standard 2001,* CD–ROM. Redmond, Wash.: Microsoft Corporation, 2001.

"Italy." *Microsoft Encarta Encyclopedia Standard 2001,* CD–ROM. Redmond, Wash.: Microsoft Corporation, 2001.

"Japan." *Microsoft Encarta Encyclopedia Standard 2001,* CD–ROM. Redmond, Wash.: Microsoft Corporation, 2001.

Neft, Naomi, and Ann D. Levine. *Where Women Stand: An International Report on the Status of Women in 140 Countries 1997–1998.* New York: Random House, 1997.

"New Zealand." *Microsoft Encarta Encyclopedia Standard 2001,* CD–ROM. Redmond, Wash.: Microsoft Corporation, 2001.

"Nigeria." *Microsoft Encarta Encyclopedia Standard 2001,* CD–ROM. Redmond, Wash.: Microsoft Corporation, 2001.

"Poland." *Microsoft Encarta Encyclopedia Standard 2001,* CD–ROM. Redmond, Wash.: Microsoft Corporation, 2001.

Ponce de Leon, Maria. *Lecture on Educational Structures in Italy.* Rome: American University of Rome, spring 2000.

Primary Education in India. Washington, D.C.: World Bank, 1997.

"Russia." *Microsoft Encarta Encyclopedia Standard 2001,* CD–ROM. Redmond, Wash.: Microsoft Corporation, 2001.

Schmida, Leslie C., ed. and Deborah G. Keenum. *Education in the Middle East.* Washington, D.C.: AMIDEAST, 1997.

"South Africa." *Microsoft Encarta Encyclopedia Standard 2001,* CD–ROM. Redmond, Wash.: Microsoft Corporation, 2001.

"Spain." *Microsoft Encarta Encyclopedia Standard 2001*, CD–ROM. Redmond, Wash.: Microsoft Corporation, 2001.

Torres, Carlos Alberto, and Adriana Puiggros. *Latin American Education: Comparative Perspectives*. Boulder, Colo.: Westview Press, 1997.

Uchendu, Patrick F. *Politics and Education in Nigeria*. New York: Fourth Dimension, 1995.

UNICEF. *State of the World's Children, Annual Report* 1999.

UNICEF. S*tate of the World's Children*, Statistical Tables. 1998.

Unterhalter, Elaine, Harold Wolpe, and Thazamile Botha. *Education in a Future South Africa: Policy Issue for Transformation*. Trenton, N.J.: African World Press, 1992.

Urch, George E. F. *Education in Sub-Saharan Africa: A Source Book*. New York: Garland, 1992.

U.S. Department of Education. National Center for Education Statistics. *Digest of Education Statistics, 1999*, NCES 2000–031, by Tom Synder. Project Manager, Charlene M. Hoffman. Washington, D.C., 2000.

U.S. Department of Education. National Center for Education Statistics. *International Education Indicators: A Time Series Perspective 1985–1995*, NCES 2000–021, by Stephane Baldi, George Khalaf, Marianne Perie, and Joel D. Sherman. Project Officer, Thomas D. Synder. Washington, D.C., 2000.

U.S. Department of Education. National Center for Education Statistics. *Adult Literacy in OCED Countries: Technical Report on the First Literacy Survey*, NCES 98–053, by T. Scott Murray, Irwin S. Kirsch, and Lynn B. Jenkins. Project Officer, Marilyn Binkley. Washington, D.C., 1998.

U.S. Department of Education. National Center for Education Statistics. *Public Attitudes Towards Secondary Education: The United States in an International Context*, NCES 97–595, by Roy Pearson, Erica O'Neal, Laura Hersh Salganik, and Marilyn McMillen, Washington, D.C., 1997.

U.S. Department of Education. National Center for Education Statistics. *International Education Indicators: A Time Series Perspective*, NCES 9–059, by Marianne Perie,

Zhongren Jing, Roy Pearson, Joel D. Sherman. Project Officer, Tom Synder. Washington, D.C., 1997.

Websites:

http://ed.gov/pubs/ResearchToday/98-3038
http://monbu.go.jp
http://www.cerent.edu.cn
http://www.cmec.ca/indexe.stm
http://www.education.nic.in
http://www.statcan.ca

World Book Encyclopedia, 83rd ed., s.v. "education."

Appendix: General Statistics on Education Worldwide

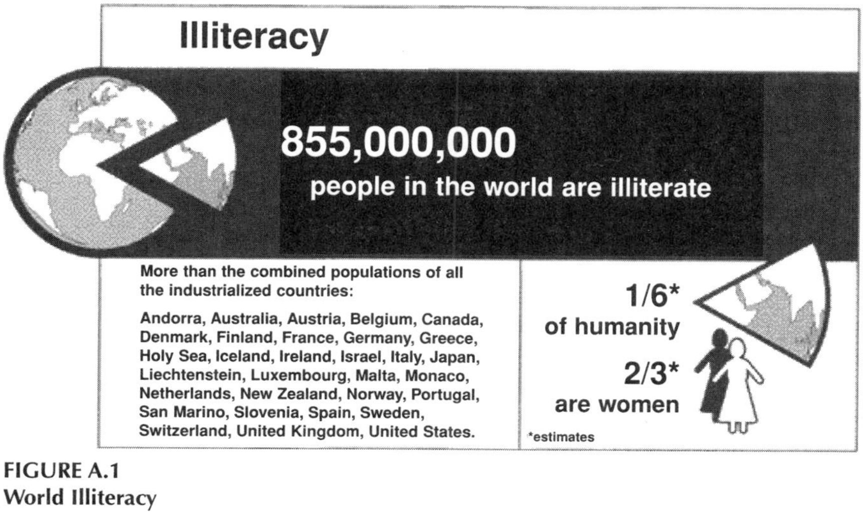

Illiteracy

855,000,000
people in the world are illiterate

More than the combined populations of all the industrialized countries:

Andorra, Australia, Austria, Belgium, Canada, Denmark, Finland, France, Germany, Greece, Holy Sea, Iceland, Ireland, Israel, Italy, Japan, Liechtenstein, Luxembourg, Malta, Monaco, Netherlands, New Zealand, Norway, Portugal, San Marino, Slovenia, Spain, Sweden, Switzerland, United Kingdom, United States.

1/6*
of humanity

2/3*
are women

*estimates

FIGURE A.1
World Illiteracy

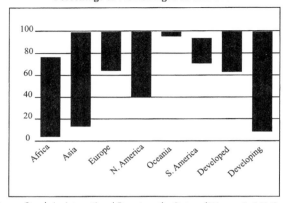

Percentage of Women Aged 15 and Over

Source: *Where Women Stand: An International Report on the Status of Women in 140 Countries 1997–1998*

FIGURE A.2
Ranges in Female Literacy

TABLE A.1
Literacy Rates

	Country	Male	Female	Total
1	United States	99%	99%	99%
2	Canada	99%	99%	99%
3	Brazil	76%	77%	85%
4	Argentina	96%	96%	96%
5	United Kingdom	99%	99%	99%
6	Italy	99%	99%	99%
7	Germany	99%	99%	99%
8	Spain	98%	98%	98%
9	Russia	99%	99%	99%
10	Poland	99%	99%	99%
11	South Africa	70%	70%	85%
12	Nigeria	63%	42%	64%
13	Iraq	68%	41%	58%
14	Egypt	66%	44%	55%
15	Israel	95%	89%	96%
16	Japan	99%	99%	99%
17	China	87%	68%	85%
18	India	64%	39%	56%
19	New Zealand	99%	99%	99%
20	Australia	99%	99%	99%

Male and Female statistics taken from *Where Women Stand: An International Report on the Status of Women in 140 Countries 1997–1998*
Total statistics taken from United Nations Education, Scientific and Cultural Organization (UNESCO)

Literacy rate is the percent of population aged 15 and over who can read and write a simple sentence about their everyday life. The literacy rate is a good measure of a country's social and economic well being. Comparing the female literacy rate with that of the males provides one measure of the status of women in a country.

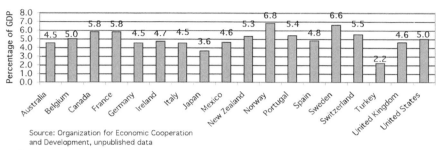

Source: Organization for Economic Cooperation and Development, unpublished data

FIGURE A.3
Public Expenditures for Education as a Percentage of the Gross Domestic Product for Selected Countries, 1995

TABLE A.2
Education Expenditure as Share of
Gross National Product

	Country	Percentage
1	South Africa (1996)	8.0
2	Poland (1996)	7.5
3	Canada (1993)	7.3
4	New Zealand (1996)	7.3
5	Israel (1993)	6.6
6	Nigeria (1981)	6.4
7	Australia (1993)	5.6
8	Egypt (1994)	5.6
9	United Kingdom (1993)	5.0
10	United States (1993)	5.3
11	Spain (1996)	5.0
12	Italy (1996)	4.9
13	Germany (1996)	4.8
14	Brazil (1989)	4.6
15	Russia (1993)	4.1
16	Iraq (19985)	4.0
17	Japan (1993)	3.8
18	Argentina (1996)	3.5
19	India (1996)	3.2
20	China (1996)	2.3

Statistics from United Nations Educational, Scientific and Cultural Organization (UNESCO)

Education expenditure as share of Gross National Product (GNP) represents the amount of government money spent on education divided by the total economic output of the country. Expenditures include funding for all levels of public education. Comparing expenditures to total GNP is useful because it compensates for differences in economic sizes among countries. Thee figure can reflect the economic value placed on education by a society. Higher percentages correspond to a greater emphasis on public education.

Compulsory education duration refers to the number of years of school attendance that is required. The purpose of compulsory education is to provide every child with some basic education. More years of compulsory education can correspond to a higher education level in a country. However, school attendance is not always possible because of factors such as shortage of teachers, schools, distance, and economic conditions that require a child to work at a young age.

Enrollment is the number of students in primary, secondary and tertiary education. In most countries, children aged six to eleven are considered of primary school age and are required by law to attend primary

TABLE A.3
Compulsory Education: Beginning and Finishing Age Duration

	Country	Beginning Age	Finishing Age	Duration
1	United States	6	16	10
2	Canada	6	16	10
3	Brazil	7	14	8
4	Argentina	5	14	10
5	United Kingdom	5	16	11
6	Italy	6	14	8
7	Germany	6	18	12
8	Spain	6	16	10
9	Russia	6	15	9
10	Poland	7	15	8
11	South Africa	6	14	9
12	Nigeria	6	12	6
13	Iraq	6	12	6
14	Egypt	6	14	8
15	Israel	5	15	11
16	Japan	6	15	9
17	China	7	15	9
18	India	6	14	8
19	New Zealand	6	16	10
20	Australia	6	15	10

*Statistics from United Nations Education, Scientific and Cultural Organization (UNESCO)

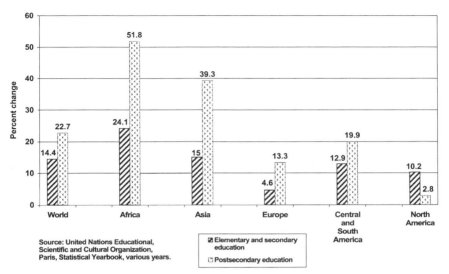

FIGURE A.4
Percent Change in Enrollment, by Area of the World and Level of Education: 1990–1996

TABLE A.4
School Enrollment Rates among Primary, Secondary, and Tertiary Schools

	Country	Primary	Secondary	Tertiary
1	United States	24,045,967	21,473,692	14,261,778
2	Canada	2, 448,144	2,505,389	1,763,105
3	Brazil	35,838,372	6,967,905	1,868,529
4	Argentina	5,153,256	2,594,329	
5	United Kingdom	5,284,125	6,548,786	1,820,849
6	Italy	2,816,128	4,602,243	1,892,542
7	Germany	3,804,887	8,382,335	2,131,907
8	Spain	2,567,012	3,852,102	1,684,445
9	Russia	7,849,000		
10	Poland	5,021,378	2,539,138	720,267
11	South Africa	8,159,430		
12	Nigeria	16,190,947		
13	Iraq	2,903,923	1,160,421	197,800
14	Egypt	7,499,303	6,726,738	
15	Israel	631,916	541,737	198,766
16	Japan	7,855,387		
17	China	139,954,000	71,883,000	6,075,215
18	India	110,390,406	68,872,393	6,060,418
19	New Zealand	357,569	433,347	169,656
20	Australia	1,855,789	2,367,692	1,041,648

*Statistics from United Nations Education, Scientific and Cultural Organization (UNESCO)

school. Secondary education includes middle schools, secondary or high schools, teacher-training schools, and vocational or technical schools. Tertiary schools include universities, teachers colleges, and professional schools. The number of students enrolled at each level is a strong indicator of a countries educational level, social trends and commitment to education.

Primary school enrollment refers to estimates of primary school age children enrolled in primary school as a proportion of the population of primary school age children. Gross enrollment ratios can exceed 100 percent in countries where students outside the normal age group attend primary school. Male and female enrollment rations can be compared to indicate relative education opportunities between the sexes.

Secondary school enrollment refers to estimates of secondary school age children enrolled in secondary school as a proportion of the population of secondary school age children. Gross enrollment ratios can exceed

TABLE A.5
Primary School Enrollment Ratio

	Country	Male	Female	Total
1	United States	102.0	100.7	101.4
2	Canada	99.7	106.0	102.8
3	Brazil	125.0	114.1	125.0
4	Argentina	113.9	112.7	113.3
5	United Kingdom	115.8	117.1	116.4
6	Italy	100.7	99.8	100.3
7	Germany	105.5	105.1	105.3
8	Spain	108.9	108.6	108.8
9	Russia	118.0	116.6	117.3
10	Poland	99.4	97.6	98.5
11	South Africa	117.3	115.2	116.3
12	Nigeria	96.7	76.5	86.6
13	Iraq	90.7	77.1	84.1
14	Egypt	108.0	94.0	101.0
15	Israel	101.0	99.8	99.3
16	Japan	101.0	101.0	101.0
17	China	122.0	123.0	123.0
18	India	110.0	90.4	100.6
19	New Zealand	101.0	101.0	101.0
20	Australia	101.0	101.0	101.0

*Statistics from United Nations Education, Scientific and Cultural Organization (UNESCO)

TABLE A.6
Secondary School Enrollment Ratio

	Country	Male	Female	Total
1	United States	96.8	97.8	97.3
2	Canada	108.1	107.2	107.7
3	Brazil	42.4	56.8	62.0
4	Argentina	72.9	80.9	76.8
5	United Kingdom	122.2	143.5	132.5
6	Italy	90.6	91.1	90.8
7	Germany	102.7	100.8	101.8
8	Spain	119.1	134.0	126.3
9	Russia	82.0	89.0	85.5
10	Poland	96.8	96.7	96.7
11	South Africa	76.5	91.4	83.9
12	Nigeria	37.0	31.1	34.0
13	Iraq	49.8	31.9	41.1
14	Egypt	83.0	73.0	78.0
15	Israel	89.1	87.4	88.3
16	Japan	105.3	106.9	106.1
17	China	74.0	66.0	70.0
18	India	58.7	39.2	49.3
19	New Zealand	110.0	116.0	113.0
20	Australia	150.0	155.0	153.0

*Statistics from United Nations Education, Scientific and Cultural Organization (UNESCO)

100 percent in countries where students outside the normal age group attend secondary school. The gross enrollment ratio provides one measure of the number of children who attain more than a basic education, and the educational trends in a given country. Male and female enrollment ratios can be compared to indicate relative education opportunities between the sexes.

Tertiary school enrollment is the number of people enrolled in universities, teachers colleges, and professional schools. The statistic expresses the figure as a percentage of the total population of relevant age. It is calculated by dividing the number of people in tertiary schools by the total population of relevant age, then multiplying the result by 100. Tertiary enrollment measures a country's educational trends, including its commitment to advanced education. Comparing male and female enrollment ratios can reveal differences in educational opportunities among the sexes.

TABLE A.7
Tertiary School Enrollment Ratio

	Country	Male	Female	Total
1	United States	77.0	91.3	80.6
2	Canada	82.7	97.8	90.1
3	Brazil	10.8	12.6	11.7
4	Argentina	37.3	46.4	41.8
5	United Kingdom	48.1	52.8	50.4
6	Italy	39.3	46.3	42.7
7	Germany	48.1	42.3	45.3
8	Spain	47.0	55.3	51.1
9	Russia	36.9	46.0	41.4
10	Poland	20.9	27.8	24.3
11	South Africa	19.6	18.0	18.8
12	Nigeria	5.7	2.2	4.0
13	Iraq	13.3	8.5	10.9
14	Egypt	27.1	17.8	22.6
15	Israel	41.2	46.0	43.6
16	Japan	46.5	38.7	42.7
17	China	7.3	3.9	6.0
18	India	8.4	5.2	6.9
19	New Zealand	53.0	73.0	63.0
20	Australia	77.0	83.0	80.0

*Statistics from United Nations Education, Scientific and Cultural Organization (UNESCO)

Index

About the Authors

Rita J. Simon is a sociologist who earned her doctorate at the University of Chicago in 1957. Before coming to American University in 1983 to serve as dean of the School of Justice, she was a member of the faculty at the University of Illinois, at the Hebrew University of Jerusalem, and the University of Chicago. She is currently university professor in the School of Public Affairs and the Washington College of Law at American University.

Professor Simon has authored thirty-one books and edited seventeen, including *Adoption Across Borders* with Howard Altstein (2000), *In the Golden Land: A Century of Russian and Soviet Jewish Immigration* (1997), *The Ambivalent Welcome: Media Coverage of American Immigration* with Susan Alexander (1993), and *New Lives: The Adjustements of Soviet Jewish Immigrants in the United States and Israel* (1985).

She is currently the editor of *Gender Issues*. She served, from 1978 to 1981, as editor of *The American Sociological Review* and, from 1983 to 1986, as editor of *Justice Quarterly*. In 1966 she received a Guggenheim Fellowship.

Lisa Banks is an attorney with the law firm of Bernabei & Katz in Washington, D.C., specializing in representing plaintiffs in employment, civil rights, and civil liberties matters. She received her B.A. from Trinity College in Hartford, Connecticut in 1990 and her J.D. from the University of Denver College of Law in 1995. Ms. Banks was an editor of the *Denver University Law Review* and clerked for judges on the Colorado Court of Appeals and Colorado Supreme Court from 1995 to 1997. Ms. Banks served as an appellate attorney with the Office of General Counsel of the U.S. Equal Employment Opportunity Commission from 1997 to 2000. In 1999, Ms. Banks accepted an offer to spend six months as an attorney advisor in the Office of the Counsel to the President in the White House. She has authored numerous appellate briefs and argued cases in the United States Courts of Appeal for the Third, Fourth, Fifth, Sixth, Ninth, Tenth and Eleventh Circuits.

Ms. Banks published an article in the *Denver University Law Review* and has recently coauthored two articles on the Supreme Court for the *National Law Journal*. She has also done freelance writing for magazines and has edited several scholarly articles and books. Banks is currently working on a book about great women in the law in America.